Do Good to Do Better:

The Small Business Guide to Growing Your Business by Helping Nonprofits

Sheryl Green

ISBN: 978-1-7323311-4-3

"The purpose of this life is to live a life of purpose."

- Wookiefoot

Acknowledgments

There is such a wealth of knowledge in this book, and honestly, a great deal of it came from other people. In addition to all the fabulous books and articles I drew upon, I couldn't have done this without Ed Chansky, Gina Bongiovi, Jess Todtfeld, Geoff Radcliffe, and Erin Gargan King.

I'm forever grateful for the support of my amazing friends and family. Thank you to my parents for cheering me on and eagerly pointing out examples of Cause Marketing after they learned what to look for. Thank you to my beta readers, Joe Wittenwiler, Ronen Rahaman, and Adam Kent for dealing with the first draft. Thank you to my entire launch team for providing feedback before it hit the shelves, and thank you to David Wiener for allowing me to "not be fun" while I put the final touches on the book.

Special thanks to Taryn Wittenwiler for keeping my commas under control and Brandon Wayne for the phenomenal cover.

Finally, thank you to my dog, Akasha. I couldn't write without frequent puppy breaks.

Hearts Alive Village Las Vegas

Thank you for purchasing <u>Do Good to Do Better: The Small Business Guide to Growing Your Business by Helping Nonprofits</u>. 10% from the sale of every book will go to support the life-saving programs at Hearts Alive Village, a 501(c)3 animal rescue in Las Vegas, NV.

HAVLV began in 2014 after Christy Stevens (Founder) read her daughter's English journal. Ten-year-old Kendall said if she had one wish, "I'd have 10 acres of land and I would have a small animal foundation called 'Hearts Alive.' We would rescue animals from dogs to pigs."

The rescue is a few pigs short, but at the time of this printing, Hearts Alive Village (HAVLV) has saved 2,875 dogs and cats (and a few bunnies) from being lost in our shelter system. The rescue feeds approximately 300 pets in low-income homes each month, and has provided humane education to more than 1,000 children.

Your purchase has allowed us to save even more animals. For more information on how to get involved, please visit www.havlv.com.

HAV LV,

Contents

Introduction

"What if greater happiness, more meaningful impact, and increased profit are ALL surprisingly interconnected?"

- Yank Silver, Founder of Maverick1000

A few weeks before I started writing this book, I attended a speaking conference. Speakers from all over the world converged on Las Vegas to learn about not just the craft of speaking, but also the business.

One of the sessions involved a well-respected business coach who'd pull up an attendee's website on the computer and rip it to shreds (with the purpose of making it better). This experience is a bit rough for the attendee whose business is laid bare in front of the crowd, but it's incredibly helpful for both them and everyone else in the audience who can learn general lessons from the experience.

During one particular Hot Seat, the attendee stood up and described the following dilemma in her business:

"I'm a woman's leadership speaker and coach... but I also want to save the wild cats. I'm not sure how to make the two work together."

The speaker (whom I respect greatly and have worked with on multiple projects) gave the following advice:

"Forget that cat thing. People don't buy 'saving cats.' They buy leadership consulting. Stick that in a closet. When you make enough money, you can donate anything you want to the cats."

To say that I was horrified is an understatement. I think I even clutched my imaginary pearls. I kept my mouth shut during the conference, but that advice kept echoing in my head. It kept me up for two nights straight before I finally emailed the attendee. I'm including the exact email I sent her.

Dear Attendee,

I wanted to comment on something that happened this week. You asked *speaker* about integrating your love of big cat preservation into your business and he told you no.

Let me first say that I respect him immensely and that I have not achieved anywhere near the level of success that he has (yet!). That being said, I see things differently.

Cause Marketing and conscious capitalism are here and they are not going anywhere anytime soon. Having

something you care about sets you apart from the competition when you utilize it properly.

My suggestion is that instead of shoving a part of yourself into a closet in order to make money, you lean into it, embrace it, and rock it.

Cats are a symbol of feminism. Big cats are a symbol of power and strength. If you branded yourself around Big Cat Leadership (or something like that), you could call attention to the traits that make women such powerful leaders while aligning yourself with an amazing cause. Additionally, you could donate a portion of your profits to whatever nonprofit you support, and use your platform to not only sell your brand of leadership, but also lend awareness to a population that has no voice and that needs our support. If it sounds interesting, run it by some of your clients to see if it gels with them.

I hope this helps or at least gets you thinking. I doubt you'd tell your women leaders to squash a piece of their identity, but rather, embrace what makes them different, special, and a force to be reckoned with.

When I began researching this book, I intended to write a guide to Cause Marketing for small businesses (don't worry, I'll define that term shortly). But the more I read, the more I studied, and the more I observed the problems that we're experiencing in our world today, I realized that this book is about much more than point-of-sale campaigns.

Let's talk about your business for a moment. Hopefully, you're doing pretty well out there. You provide a good product or service, treat your customers right, and if you have employees, they're pretty happy. You are, however, probably facing a few of these challenges:

1) The market is saturated. You can probably list at least five other people or companies that do what you do.

2) Advertising is expensive and while social media may be the answer to everything, it's also everyone's answer to everything. Every single platform is virtually saturated.

3) You're tired of competing on price. Attempting to undercut your competition is devaluing what you do and making it difficult to provide the level of service you want to provide.

4) You work in one of those industries that's hard to sell. People don't want to think about what you do.

5) You've recently had long-term, happy customers who got distracted by the newest shiny object on the market and switched to another brand.

6) You don't like some of your customers. It's okay to admit this. When you are working with the wrong clients, work can be downright painful.

7) Your employees are going through the motions at work. You can tell that if a better opportunity presented itself, they'd jump ship.

You aren't alone. Thousands of small- to medium-sized business owners have felt these pressures. In fact, corporations have felt these pressures (though on a much larger scale) for years. The difference is they (some of them at least) know how to handle it.

This book is about adopting the principles that big corporations have understood and utilized for decades, and applying those principles to a small- to medium-sized business or solopreneurship.

Imagine if someone had told Blake Mycoskie, founder of TOMS Shoes, "Don't worry about that whole kids-without-shoes thing. Just make enough money and you can donate whatever you want to them."

Imagine if someone told Yvon Chouinard, founder of the outdoor supply company Patagonia, "No one buys saving the environment. Just make enough money and then you can plant a few trees."

I believe that as business owners, we have both the power and the responsibility to change the world we live in. We can either embrace that power and harness it to create change while improving our businesses, or we can shove the very qualities that set us apart into a closet and sit back as our world crumbles before our very eyes.

Now, how's that for a call to action?

"Businesses must reconnect company success with social progress. Shared value is not social responsibility, philanthropy, or even sustainability, but a new way to achieve economic success. It is not on the margin of what companies do but at the center." - Michael Porter, Founder of FSG, a social impact consulting firm

Section One:

What is Cause Marketing and Why Do I Need It?

Chapter One: The Problems at Hand

Warning: The first few paragraphs of this chapter are going to be a bit of a bummer. You have my word that it will get better! Just stick with me and I promise it will be alright.

I'm not sure if you've noticed, but we've got a few problems in this world. Whether you subscribe to a specific political party, or whether you're hiding under a rock like me (it's cozy under here), you've probably noticed that we're facing some challenges.

For many, many years, we've put our trust in the government to fix societal issues. Most people sat back and thought, "It's okay, that's what the government is here for."

And yet... There are homeless people on almost every street corner; a staggering percentage of children are considered "food insecure;" babies are dying because they don't have access to clean water and vaccinations; companion animals are being killed in our shelters because there aren't enough homes for all of them; veterans - men and women who have served our country and fought for our freedom - are living in pay-by-the-week motels and eating packaged ramen noodles; and our environment is turning into a port-a-potty on the last day of a weeklong music festival.

Nice job, government. Keep up the good work!

I'm still petitioning to add a sarcasm font, but I'm pretty sure you get the gist of what I'm saying.

Our world is hurting right now.

James E. Austin, author of The Collaboration Challenge said,

> No longer can society look to the federal government as the main problem solver. Trust in government and politicians has diminished; the limits of the state have been acknowledged. This has triggered a massive devolution of social functions from the federal to local levels and from the public to the private sector. The shifting of responsibilities is greatly increasing the demands on the nonprofit and business sectors and pushing them toward collaboration.

And if you have a "damn rich people are just trying to get out of paying taxes" mentality... don't feel bad, I did too. Until, that is, I watched an interview with John Paul DeJoria, co-founder of Paul Mitchell Hair Care Systems and my new hero.

John Paul pointed out that the government hasn't been doing the best job of keeping our world running smoothly. So, is it a terrible thing if the wealthy people (like him and Richard Branson and Bill Gates) try to limit the amount of taxes they pay, and instead, set up foundations to focus directly on societal issues (which they've done) and stamp them out once and for all?

Would you like to join me in a round of "Daaaaaaamn."

I hadn't thought of that. Sure, taxes are important, but why are we mad at rich people for not throwing money into a broken system, when many of them are attacking these problems from a different, and likely better, angle?

There's a good chance that at this point, you're sitting back and thinking, "Sheryl, this is all well and good, but what does it have to do with me?"

I'm glad you asked that question.

You are a small business (or a nonprofit). Chances are that you got into business to help people (or animals) and to make this world a better place. But you may have subscribed to the school of thought we discussed in the Introduction: make your money and then do good.

This is old-school thinking and I'm going to present oodles of research in the coming chapters that will convince you that I'm not alone in this belief.

Research aside, I'm not sure how old you are or what stage you're in with your business, but I'm nearing 40 and still in the early stages of my entrepreneurial journey. I don't want to wait another 10-20 years to start making a difference in this world.

Instead of sitting back and waiting for the money to roll in so we can support the causes close to our hearts, I believe that when we support the causes close to our hearts... the money will roll in.

Go ahead, re-read that. I know it's a subtle difference, but it's a very important one.

> Unfortunately, many people think they can't give anything away when they start a business because they have nothing to give. Nor, they fear, can they share a percentage of their profits because they don't have any profits yet. But that's the very reason you should do it. Without resources, you will need a lot of other people's help. And the best way to get that help is to stand for something bigger than just yourself and your business. (Blake Mycoskie, founder of TOMS Shoes)

All right, before we get any further, you're probably wondering who I am and why I'm writing this book. Let me give you a quick rundown so you can rest assured that you're in good hands for this journey.

As a teenager and twentysomething, I wanted to catch serial killers. I was obsessed with what made criminals tick. So I went to undergrad for a degree in Psychology and did a second major in Anthropology because it was cool and meant that I got to study in Greece for a month.

Once I was finished with my Bachelor's, I decided that my best course of action to get into the FBI and become a Profiler was to get a Master's Degree in Forensic Psychology. I did. Of course, getting into the FBI proved to be more difficult than I originally imagined.

I only applied once. I failed the polygraph test on the "Are you a terrorist" question. In hindsight, it was a blessing. I can't even imagine working in that kind of environment and spending my days looking at the absolute worst of humanity.

Unsure of what I wanted to be when I grew up now that my original plan had proven faulty, I drifted from customer service job to customer service job.

And then in 2008, I moved out to Las Vegas after a horrendous divorce. I won't get into the details here, but if you'd like to learn more, read my first book, Surviving to Thriving: How to Overcome Setbacks and Rock Your Life.

What you need to know for the purpose of this book is that I went through a pretty severe clinical depression after the divorce. My rock bottom moment came on the floor of the bathroom. I was living with my dad and my stepmom at the time and they came home to find me curled up in the fetal position, bawling onto the cold tiles. My stepmom picked me up, sat me down on the couch, and gave me the best piece of advice anyone can ever get:

"Go do something for someone else."

For me, those "someones" happened to be animals. I began volunteering with animal rescues. Over the course of five years, I met my tribe: friends that have become family because we share a common mission in life. I've discovered skills that I had no idea I possessed and found mentors to teach me skills I had no idea that I needed. I landed an internship with a PR company and learned the ropes of Public Relations. I got jobs through my rescue connections, and eventually, got the universal kick in the butt that caused me to start my own business. And I realized that when it comes to animals... I have no shame. Like none. I will ask anyone for absolutely anything if it means that I get to save a dog or cat. I used to be an introvert. That's gone the way of the dodo bird. Rescue has changed who I am, down to my core.

As the job opportunities and then clients began to roll in, I realized that volunteering didn't just have the benefit of reshaping personal lives. It also had the power to ignite business opportunities.

I've spent years with my hand held out asking for donations. And to be perfectly honest, it gets old after a while. I don't remember the exact moment that I stumbled on the term Cause Marketing, but I'm fairly sure the sun shone a spotlight on whatever I was reading, a choir of angels began to sing, and I jumped on the idea like my dog jumps on her chew toy when she realizes it's in the room.

I co-founded an event called Businesses with Heart and eventually parlayed that into the Cause Marketing Chamber of Commerce, an organization that educates and fosters relationships between businesses and nonprofits to improve sales, visibility, and our community as a whole.

Hopefully no one will ever find the video, but in middle school I sang Michael Jackson's "Heal the World"... in French. I guess the drive has always been inside me.

Businesses and nonprofits working together for a greater good... I can picture the kumbaya around the campfire as we all toast marshmallows to celebrate how perfect our world is.

Okay, we're not there yet; but my hope, my goal, is that by the time you finish reading this book, you'll stand up, raise your fist to the sky, and scream, "Hellz yeah! We're gonna fix the world!"

Sheryl, aren't you a bit overly optimistic?

Yeah. I've been called worse. Before we jump into Chapter Two and I actually tell you what all this Cause Marketing talk is about, I'll leave you with a quote from Steve Jobs:

"Those who are crazy enough to think they can change the world usually do."

Chapter Two: What is Cause Marketing?

"Remember, you vote with your wallet. Your dollar bill's your ballot. Alone it's just a whisper, but together you can't stop it."

- Wookiefoot, a band and nonprofit charity organization

Just for a moment, I'd like you to take your business-owner hat off and put on your consumer hat.

Did you do it? Good.

Have you ever, or would you ever, stop doing business with a company that behaved in a manner you didn't agree with? Maybe they took advantage of their employees; tested their products on cute, furry animals; dumped toxic sludge into our water supply; or alienated a section of the population.

I know I have.

Let's take a look at the other side of that coin. Would you be willing to start (or continue) doing business with a company because they support a cause or stand for something that you agree with?

Welcome to Cause Marketing.

You can put your business-owner hat back on now. In Path to Purpose, Carolyn Butler-Madden describes Cause Marketing:

> When a brand aligns itself with a cause to drive social impact and create brand value. An authentic alignment between a brand and its selected cause partner allows the brand to develop a credible social purpose. This is then marketed in a way that enables the brand's customers, consumers, its company's employees and partners, and even the wide public, to become collaborators in creating social impact around that purpose.

I like to describe it as, "selling warm fuzzies instead of widgets."

There's some confusion over where the term (and the practice) of Cause Marketing originated. It appears that the actual practice began in 1979 when Wally Amos, founder of Famous Amos cookies, became the National Spokesperson for the Literacy Volunteers of America. The term, however, is attributed to American Express, which launched a campaign to renovate the Statue of Liberty.[1]

Wherever it originated, and whether the term sticks or not, the practice of businesses working with nonprofits is here to stay. So come out of the closet and wave your passion freely. In the next chapter, we'll discuss that there is even a myriad of benefits you'll receive from aligning yourself with a cause.

But before we get too much further into this discussion, I'd like to address the term "Give back." This term gets passed around more than a joint at a Ziggy Marley concert and I think it's time we finally ditched it.

By very definition, in order to "give back," you have to first take something.

Right?

Remember when you were a kid playing Barbies or GI Joe with your friends? Your friend would snatch a toy out of your hand and you'd scream, "Mooooooooom! He took my toy! I wasn't done playing with it." You'd start to cry and your mom would come stomping into the room like Godzilla, eyes red and steam coming out of her nose. "Give. Timmy. Back. His. Toy," she'd say in that voice that caused the hair on the back of your neck to stand up. Your friend would toss the toy at you and run out of the room because he pretty much peed his pants.

That is what I think of when I hear the term "give back."

If you haven't taken anything, why would you be giving something back?

Now, I can't speak for you, but in my business, I provide a service (writing, speaking, or consulting) in return for money. I do not coerce or manipulate my clients into working with me and I do not take anything that I have not earned. Therefore, I feel no compulsion to "give back."

What I will do, is give forward. I will share the money that I have made and the skills that I have developed in order to make this world a better place.

So please, if you have not taken anything from people, please stop "giving back." Give forward and let's change the discussion from one of scarcity, to one where everyone wins.

Chapter Three: The Benefits of Cause Marketing

When I teach my "Storytelling for Business" workshops, I like to start out with a call and response game. Let's do it here (though if you're sitting in a coffee shop, you may not want to yell it out, as people will think you're insane).

People do business with people they _____, _____, and _____.

Did you yell it out?

People do business with people they *know, like,* and *trust.*

I then walk my students through the stories that will help them gain the "Know, Like, and Trust" factors with potential clients. Do you know what story helps establish two of those?

If you just mouthed "the Cause Marketing story," please give yourself a pat on the back. We'll discuss storytelling later in the book, but for now, let's discuss how Cause Marketing can help you build "know" and "like" with your potential customers. Going this route isn't necessarily the fastest way to bring in a customer; however, if you're looking to establish a positive brand for your company and forge long-term relationships with loyal customers that become an army of adoring fans, this is the way to go.

Let's back up a little bit. What is "marketing"?

Dictionary.com defines marketing as, "the action or business of promoting and selling products or services, including market research and advertising."

And what's the goal of marketing? Say it with me now,

"To get your brand in front of people."

Let's talk about brand, baby! (I'd write some Salt-n-Pepa lyrics here, but I don't want to get sued.)

All of your years in business and on this planet, you've probably looked at brand as how a business wants to be seen.

Buzzer sounds: WRONG

I'm about to blow your mind so I hope you're sitting. A brand is actually how your *audience* sees you based on your actions.

Go ahead, comb your hair back down and take a deep breath. I know. It's a lot to sink in. In case you're having a problem grasping the concept, let me give you a quick example.

Let's say you own a gym. The brand you've chosen is "open 24/7 and readily accessible to make it easier for the customer to work out no matter what time of day or night they feel the urge."

Great business idea.

Now, let's imagine that the key fob your gym-goers need to get into the facility doesn't work. On top of that, your customer service is so horrific, that instead of being met with cheerful assistance when presenting a challenge, your customer is met with apathy and the response, "I'm not even supposed to be here today!"

Yes, this actually happened.

Yes, I had an immediate flashback to the movie <u>Clerks</u>.

This gym's brand is no longer "easily accessible and pleasant to work out at." Instead, the experience (and the brand image in my mind) embodies the phrase, "You can't argue with apathy."

Was this what they were shooting for? Probably not.

Is this the way that I talk about the gym in conversation? Yup.

Does the concept make sense now? Brand is not what you decide you want to be known for. Brand is what your customers decide you'll be known for.

So what exactly are the benefits of Cause Marketing? For now, we're going to discuss the benefits to for-profits (we'll focus on nonprofits a little bit later).

Improved Brand Awareness

Now that you know what a brand really is, Cause Marketing is a great way to not only get your name out into the world, but to also have a deeper purpose associated with it.

"Marketers need to think less about what their brand can say about itself in order to be relevant and start thinking more about what their brand can do for the world we live in." - Butler-Madden, Path to Purpose

Attract Your Tribe

Do you enjoy doing business with people you don't like?

I know I don't. The beauty of building a business is that as you get busier, you have the option to filter out the customers you don't want to work with. Maybe they have drastically different political views (and spout them unnecessarily), maybe they have different morals than you, or maybe they're just a PITA.

On the flip side, isn't it easier to work with and communicate with people who have similar beliefs, concerns, interests, etc.? When you find that common ground with someone, a new level of relationship blossoms:

"OMG, you're from Long Island? I'm from Long Island!" "No! You love puppies? I love puppies, too!"

What if you had a surefire way to filter out the people you don't want to work with and attract more of the people you do?

In Tribes, Seth Godin (a marketing genius) discusses the importance of attracting like-minded people to you. "A tribe is a group of people connected to one another, connected to a leader, and connected to an idea."

The idea, in this case, being that we can fix a societal problem. When you attach yourself and your business to a cause, you attract like-minded individuals. People you actually want to work with.

It's Now Expected

Love them or hate them, Millennials are not going anywhere. They are consumers; they've entered the workforce; and they want to change the world. In fact, Gen Z is close behind them and they want to work for and buy from businesses that are making a difference in our communities, too. (More on these consumer groups in a bit.)

According to Deloitte's 2017 Global Millennial survey:

- 76% of Millennials now regard business as a force for positive social impact.
- 88% of Millennials say business, in general, around the world is having a positive impact on the wider society in which it operates.

The 2017 Cone Cause Evolution Study found that:

- 80% of Millennials believe companies have the obligation to help people or take actions to improve issues that may not be related to their everyday business.
- 85% of Millennials will seek out responsible products whenever possible.

And it's not just Millennials. According to the 2018 Edelman Brand study: nearly two-thirds (64 percent) of consumers around the world will buy or boycott a brand solely because of its position on a social or political issue; a staggering increase of 13 points from last year.[2]

Differentiate Yourself from the Competition

When I work with a website client, one of my first questions is always, "What makes you different from the next (fill in the business)?"

The first round of answers usually goes something like this:

"We focus on customer service, really going out of our way for our customers."

Or

"We have high-quality products."

Or (my personal favorite),

"We are very communicative. We respond to emails, phone calls, FB messages..."

Have you ever spent any time in the online dating world? I have, and while there are some quality folks out there, I could write a book about the Island of Misfit Men that I've met through those sites.

Let me give you an analogy based on those experiences: Saying that your business is focused on quality, customer service, and actually getting back to people is like putting, "I have a job, a car, and I no longer live in my grandma's basement" in your dating profile.

This. Is. The. Bare. Minimum.

If your customer service is a joke, your product is terrible, and you don't respond to phone calls or emails, please put down this book and go fix your business. No amount of working with a nonprofit can help you if you suck.

Phew! Sorry to get a little hardcore on you there but it had to be said.

Now, assuming that your business does not suck, what makes you different?

I recently ran into my friend Bryce at a pet event where he had a booth. He is the founder of No Kill Las Vegas and has dedicated his life to protecting animals. Bryce is also the Las Vegas Realtor to the Dogs... and their families. (www.realtortothedogs.com)

I stepped to the side when a woman stopped to snag some swag off his table.

"Do you have any friends that are looking to buy or sell a home?" he asked.

She didn't even look up, "I do. But I also know about 25 realtors."

"Do you know any that will donate $500 to the animal rescue of your choice?"

Now she looked up. "Seriously?"

Bryce nodded and the woman took a handful of his cards. Bryce just reaped the benefit of being different.

I spend a lot of time networking and if I got a dollar for every realtor, insurance agent, Network marketer, and business coach that I met... I could retire to Maui in a few weeks.

There are hundreds of people who do what you do... so what makes you different?

You, my Cause Marketing friend, stand for more than just business. You have a greater mission. You support a cause and that is your selling point.

You'll Get Improved Visibility

How many people follow you on your business Facebook page? How about Instagram? Do you have a mailing list?

When you add these numbers up (and figure for crossover between platforms), the answer you come up with is your Audience. For a small business or solopreneur, I'm going to give you the benefit of the doubt here and say that you've got 1-2k followers. And I'm being really generous here.

As of this morning, Hearts Alive Village Animal Rescue (the rescue I volunteer with and donate to) has 10,347 followers on Facebook. If a nonprofit has been building its audience for a few years, it should have numbers close to this.

Now, would you like to be seen by an extra 10,000 people? We'll discuss selecting your cause in a later chapter, but theoretically, many fellow believers will be in the market (at some point) for what you offer, so you are looking at thousands of potential customers you can connect with.

Not too shabby.

Of course, there's also the free PR that you can get when you work with a nonprofit. I'm only familiar with the local shows in Las Vegas at the moment; however, a 7-minute spot on shows like "The Morning Blend" will cost a company approximately $700. When you are working with a nonprofit... it's free.

You Can Charge (A Little Bit) More

Two years ago, I was flipping through the latest Yoga Journal magazine when I came across the cutest t-shirts. They had yogic images and phrases on them, and I wanted them in my life.

I popped over to their website and had to lie down for a moment after I saw the price... $79... for a t-shirt.

When the dizziness passed, I bounced around their website frantically looking for a cause. "Surely, they must be donating a portion of the t-shirt sale to build drinking wells in Africa, teach yoga to inner-city youth, or save the spotted lion," I mumbled as I surfed.

Nothing.

Here's the thing: had there been a donation associated with my purchase, I may have been able to stomach paying almost 80 bucks for a t-shirt. However, if that money is just going to make the owners of this company richer - oh, hell no.

Now, take a look at www.sevenly.org. Most of their t-shirts cost around $36 - a tad expensive if you compare them to shopping at a store like Old Navy; but, for every t-shirt they sell, $7 goes to a charity. In fact, when I reached out to the company, they told me that they've donated $6 million since their founding in 2011. Now I don't mind spending a bit more for a t-shirt.

When you engage in Cause Marketing and connect with a nonprofit, customers are willing to pay more for your product. In Path to Purpose, the author William Damon discusses a collaboration between Pampers and UNICEF to eliminate Maternal and Neonatal Tetanus (MNT) from the world. This disease occurs when mothers are subjected to unhygienic conditions during childbirth. However, it's easily preventable with a simple vaccine. Since its launch in 2006, 500,000 babies have been saved, 300 million vaccines have been given, and MNT has been eliminated in 17 countries.

Damon notes, "This Pampers initiative offers up a shining example of how a brand can stand for something - credibly and authentically. In doing so, Pampers has become an educator and an activist."

Pampers increased their market share despite not being the least expensive diaper on the shelves. How?

Ultimately, Damon found that, "Cause Marketing can trump lowest price. Pampers still had to be competitive on product features, but the campaign enabled the brand to emotionally connect with its consumers and gave them a compelling reason, beyond price, to choose Pampers nappies over competing products."

Accenture's From Marketing to Mattering study showed that 71% of consumers said they'd be willing to pay more for a socially and environmentally responsible product.[16]

Your Product will be Chosen over Other Brands When Quality is Comparable

Go ahead and put that consumer hat back on for a moment. You are standing in the store holding two different brands of widgets (why you're buying widgets, I don't know.... I'm not even sure where one purchases widgets).

Anyway, you have two different brands in your hands. You've used both of them before and they deliver approximately the same benefits to you. They're also in the same price range.

 The only difference is that one of them supports the endangered Spotted Haitian Sea Squirrel, where the other one just appears to do what it's intended to do.

 Which do you choose?

Well, if you have a soft spot for the endangered Spotted Haitian Sea Squirrel or any animal for that matter, you're probably going to choose that product.

Unilever released results in 2017 from an international study that asked 20,000 adults from five different countries how their purchasing decisions were impacted by their sustainability concerns. Twenty-one percent of those surveyed said they'd "more actively choose brands if they made their sustainability credentials clear on their packaging and their marketing."

My friend Joe does mortgages (mrjoelender.com). He has always donated to charity and volunteered, but he's now truly embraced the concept of Cause Marketing.

Through his local Rotary Club, he supports a program called Happy Feet. (There are no penguins. I was confused at first, as well.) The group supplies brand-new shoes to less fortunate children throughout the valley.

A few weeks ago, he was walking through a deal with a potential client. The paperwork was drawn up but the woman was hesitant to sign.

"I've also been working with someone at Chase. I'm not sure which one of you I want to go with."

"Chase is a great company, as well. You won't go wrong with either one of us. However, when you close a mortgage with me, I donate five pairs of shoes to kids in need."

The woman picked up the pen and signed.

Inspire Brand Loyalty

When I was in elementary school, I got into a tiny bit of trouble with my grades. I was an excellent student, so this probably meant going from an A to a B+, but whatever. My parents decided that I was watching too much television and it was no longer an option.

This was probably the best punishment ever because it sparked my lifelong love of reading. Granted, I'm not sure that *The Baby-Sitter's Club* and *Sweet Valley High* can be considered great literature, but I was going through books like an elephant goes through peanuts.

There were three reasons for this:

1) I loved reading;
2) I wasn't allowed to watch TV so there wasn't much else for me to do; and, the biggest reason,
3) At the time, Pizza Hut had a program called Book It! to encourage kids to read more. The more books you read, the more pizza you got.

Now I don't know if you're quite as food motivated as I am, but I do love me some pizza. My mom and I were at Pizza Hut 1-2 times per week cashing in my free pizza vouchers.

I grew up in NY, home of the most amazing pizza on the planet (relax, Chicagoans. It's home of the best NY pizza. You can still claim the best Chicago-style). Yet, I was frequenting Pizza Hut. I was loyal.

In Good Works, the authors discuss the General Mills Box Tops for Education program. I'm sure you've seen it. When you buy cereal or other General Mills products, you can choose the school you'd like to support, then cut off the proof of purchase and mail it in. General Mills donates ten cents from each box top to your chosen educational institution.

From 1996 to 2011, the program raised over $400 million for more than 90,000 elementary and middle schools. And, it was quite the marketing move for General Mills. Good Works recounted that, "Fifty-one percent of program participants indicated the BTFE made 'me stay more loyal to participating brands than I otherwise would be,' and 27% said the program influenced them to switch brands, according to a 2011 study."

You Make the Customer a Hero

We'll discuss storytelling in a later chapter but, for now, let's just talk about the most basic human characteristics. This may come as a shock to you, but we humans like to avoid pain. I know, I just totally blew your mind.

Think about it: for the most part, people don't appreciate emotional or physical pain and we are damn good at ignoring stimuli that would cause such pain. I'll throw myself under the bus with an example.

I love animals. I wish I were a vegetarian, but my body has other plans. I've tried it a few times and I felt awful and had no energy. It makes me horribly sad to think that I'm hurting animals, so despite everything I know about factory farming, I push it out of my head.

I'm not proud of this. It's guilt that I live with on a daily basis; so, I do my best not to think about it. I just want you to understand that when we can't handle the truth about something, we often just ignore it.

There's a psychological phenomenon called Collapse of Compassion. First proposed by Paul Slovic and Deborah Small, it suggests that as the number of people in need of help increased, the amount of compassion people feel toward the needy decreased.
(https://en.wikipedia.org/wiki/Collapse_of_compassion)

I'd suggest that the same proves true for animals, environmental challenges, etc.

As humans, we simply can't handle mass suffering when we can't do anything about it. So instead of feeling terrible all the time, we emotionally harden ourselves to the situation.

When you saw your first homeless person, your heart probably broke a little bit. No shoes, dirty clothing, pushing their only earthly possessions in a shopping cart, and begging for money. As compassionate individuals, we feel pain. But the more we see these people, the more hardened we become to their situation. Maybe you could give a dollar or a protein bar to one person, but the sheer number of homeless people makes it impractical to help everyone.

Okay, why did I go down this truly depressing tangent?

People want to help. Deep down (most) humans want to alleviate the suffering of other living creatures. They just don't know how.

When your business collaborates with a nonprofit, you give your customer the opportunity to be a hero.

I was at a fundraising seminar a few weeks ago and the instructor informed us that the most common reason people do not donate to charity is that they aren't asked.

I'm not sure how they've gone through life without being asked to donate to something, but I believe the statistic.

When you make it easy for someone to get involved, they'll usually help - even if it's not necessarily their cause.

Last month, I was zipping through the Wendy's drive-through on my way to visit a friend in the hospital. I ordered my hideously unhealthy lunch and was then asked, "Would you like to support Cancer Research by purchasing Frosty coupons for a dollar?"

I had good reason not to take advantage of this Point-of-Sale Cause Marketing program:

- · I've never drunk (eaten?) a Frosty and I don't think it's a necessary addition to my diet.
- · While cancer is terrible and I'd love for them to find a cure, that's not the cause that tugs on my heartstrings.

But I bought some. I've been driving around for a month now with 5 or 6 coupons for a free Frosty. Why? Because it was easy. It only cost $1 and I felt good about supporting a good cause. On a side note, I recently went through the drive-through to use a coupon for a friend and I ended up buying French fries while I was there. Was I hungry? No. Did I need French fries to survive the day? No. Did their collaboration with a nonprofit get me to re-patronize their restaurant? Sure did.

Later, we'll discuss a company called Passion Planner. For now, you just need to know that I follow them on Instagram and they totally get it:

We're working toward a better world, and we can't do it without you, #PashFam!

Cause Marketing makes it easy for your customer to become a hero.

Sexy-ify your industry

Can we be honest for a moment? There are certain industries that aren't very exciting. I chose a pretty good one, but not everyone is so lucky. When I tell people that I'm a writer, they say things like, "Ooh! What do you write?" or "Have I read anything that you've written?" They want to know more about what I do and usually confess that they've always wanted to write a book but "could never actually do it."

And then there are the poor insurance agents, funeral representatives, accountants, and other job titles that make people smile, nod, and run. I'm sorry. It's nothing personal. There are just certain industries and jobs that aren't the least bit sexy. Don't even get me started on lawyers!

When you have a cause that you and your business support, the focus is less on your actual job title and more on the difference you're making.

Improve Employee Engagement

You may not have employees if you are just starting out or running a solopreneur operation. However, if you wish to grow at some point, and eventually take a day off or a vacation, you're going to need some help.

Employee engagement is a huge buzzword these days because, frankly, most employees don't really want to be working the jobs they are working. In fact, according to a Gallup poll, only 32% of employees in the United States are engaged[3].

That means that two-thirds of all workers would rather be playing Angry Birds than doing their jobs.

Ouch.

But, if your sole purpose in life is to manufacture or market widgets... how excited can you possibly be? As a business owner, you may be super passionate about the widget industry, but you can't expect all of your staff to care.

Enter Cause Marketing or other charitable giving.

OC Tanner surveyed over 1,000 employees at companies across the United States. According to the results, "Charitable giving is not often a key focus for a company, but it should be — data from our recent research shows that organizing and promoting charitable office events can lead to enhanced employee engagement." For example, eighty-four percent of employees at companies that organized multiple holiday charitable events believe their organization has a clear purpose[4].

Don't just wait for the holidays. I'm always fascinated by how many food drives pop up around Thanksgiving and Christmas. People need to eat more than twice a year!

Incorporating giving into your company culture will improve employee engagement, make current employees happier, and allow you to attract better talent in the future.

Looking to hire millennials? Community involvement is pretty much required. According to the 2016 Cone Communications Millennial Employee Engagement Study:

- 64% of Millennials consider a company's social and environmental commitments when deciding where to work;
- 64% won't take a job if a company doesn't have strong corporate social responsibility (CSR) values;
- 83% would be more loyal to a company that helps them contribute to social and

environmental issues (vs. 70% U.S. average);
and

· 88% say their job is more fulfilling when they
are provided opportunities to make a positive
impact on social and environmental issues.[5]

Become a Brand that People are Proud to Support

Blake Mycoskie tells a story in Start Something That
Matters about a woman wearing TOMS shoes. Unaware
that she's talking to the founder of the company, the
woman is insanely excited to tell this stranger about her
shoes, what they stand for, and how by buying them, she
is helping the world.

Have you ever been that excited about an article of
clothing? When your brand stands for something beyond
its immediate function, people are eager to share their
excitement.

It's the Right Thing to Do

I work very hard to avoid any discussion of religion in any
of my books. However, I haven't found a religion, yet,
that doesn't have some aspect of donation, either to the
religious institution or to the poor. It may not be
required, but it's generally requested. Here's a quick look
at a few of them.

· Judaism: I grew up Jewish and I remember
having a little metal box to put coins in for
tzedakah (charity).

41

- Catholicism: Many Catholic churches suggest parishioners contribute 10% of their income to charity. Five percent goes to the church and 5% to a charity.
- Wicca or Paganism: No specific donation requirement; however, there is a belief that whatever you put out into the world (good or bad) comes back threefold.
- Mormonism: A 10% tithe to the church is seen as a duty and test of faithfulness.
- Islam: Zakat is obligatory tithing to the church. Sadaqah is a voluntary donation to charity.
- Hinduism and Buddhism: Both believe that the sum of your actions in this life - and previous states of existence - will determine your fate in future existences.

If you'd like to learn more (or have any questions about where I got my information, visit https://www.beliefnet.com/Freeform/Love-Family/Charity-Service/2001/04/Tithing-Chart.aspx).

However you look at it, most (if not all) major religions and belief systems advocate for some level of charity or, at least, being a good human being.

Don't believe in any of these? That's cool, too. You don't have to be afraid of eternal damnation or lifelong guilt to do what's right.

With benefits for the business owner, the employees, the customers, and the community, there's never been a better time to incorporate a cause into your business.

Have more questions? If you're willing to answer a quick survey about why you're interested in using Cause Marketing in your business, I'll give you a free 30-minute phone call where you can ask me anything (about Cause Marketing... or animal rescue... or pasta). Email me at sheryl@sherylgreenspeaks.com to schedule.

Chapter Four: Overcoming Objections

"You can't please everyone. You aren't a jar of Nutella."

- Unknown

No matter what good you do in this world, there will always be people who don't agree with you, that judge you, and that hate you because of your actions.

Harsh but true.

Now that you know you'll never make everyone happy, you can stop trying. Instead, focus on doing the most amount of good for your business and your community. Let's look at some of the misconceptions about giving to charities that may be getting in your way.

The First Rule of Cause Marketing is You Don't Talk About Cause Marketing

A few years ago, I joined a networking group called Business Network International. They encourage you to schedule one-on-one meetings to get to know the other people in your group. So just a few days after joining the chapter, I packed up my folder o' business cards and trekked out to the warehouse of the group's plumber.

He showed me around, we bonded over some pictures of his dogs, and then we began discussing Cause Marketing. His shoulders tightened and he got a bit flustered as I described the concept.

"I already give to charity."

"That's amazing! Why don't you post it on your social media?"

"Because I don't do it for the attention."

In that one sentence, my plumber friend summed up the number-one argument I face regarding Cause Marketing. He, and many others, feel that when you talk about your charity involvement, or (be still my heart!) benefit from it, it somehow takes away from the act.

I call B.S.

Let me explain it another way. I've been volunteering for animal rescues for the past ten years. As I mentioned in the Introduction, I've expanded my social circle, gotten jobs, career skills, media attention, and a whole lot of joy from working with these animals.

What I've never had is a Chihuahua stand up on his hind legs, narrow his eyes at me and say, "Excuuuuuse me! You are just getting way too much out of your time with me. I'm going to need you to calm down so I can get the lion's share of the benefits."

Nope. It's never happened. In fact, I'm pretty sure that when you actually enjoy what you're doing and (egad!) benefit from it, the other party gets more out of it as well.

Why? Because doing good is not a zero-sum game. It's not a situation where the more I get, the less you can have.

You know what else happens when you don't talk about the work you do with nonprofits?

Nothing.

Seriously. Nothing. No more money is raised for the charity. No more awareness is brought to the cause. No more people are inspired to volunteer and improve the situation. And you are missing out on one of the most powerful marketing tactics out there.

In Path to Purpose, the author discusses how REI and Patagonia actually used anti-consumerism messaging around the time of Black Friday (#optoutside) to drive increased sales.

An inordinate amount of money is spent by businesses to get people - consumers - to buy into their brand. What both REI and Patagonia have done is take a stand on an issue that is highly relevant to their category. They have used their marketing might to drive awareness of that cause and build a movement around it. In doing so, they are reawakening feelings and a belief about what is truly important to people in this world. I call that responsible marketing. I have no problem with brands like that profiting from marketing in that way and I'm not alone in that thinking.

One more thing before we blow the next B.S. misconception out of the water.

Do you remember that marketing tool that worked because no one ever heard about it?

Of course not! If you'd like to run a successful business, your desired brand better not be "Best Kept Secret." If no one knows about you, you won't stay in business. If no one knows that by doing business with you, a nonprofit will benefit, no one new will do business with you and the nonprofit will not benefit from it.

Make sense?

"I Don't Think the Money Actually Goes to the Charity"

I have to admit to a bit of naiveté in this category. You see, I live in a wonderful world with unicorns and rainbows, where people are not out to hurt one another, and no one would ever take advantage of a nonprofit who is making the world a better place.

Despite the fact that donations have been stolen multiple times from my animal rescue, I still like to believe that people are inherently good.

However, it has been brought to my attention that some people suck. They'll do anything necessary to improve their own situation, even if it means stealing from furry creatures, children, or the homeless.

In fact, as I was doing my research for this book, I came across a paragraph about Ed Chansky, an attorney (in Las Vegas) who specializes in Cause Marketing and has contributed a great deal of resources to the field.

Unicorns and rainbows prevailed and I found myself muttering, "Why would anyone need an attorney to help a nonprofit?" My dog had no answer for this, so I reached out to a lawyer friend and, one week later, I was sitting in Mr. Chansky's office learning just how bad people can be (not him, the sucky humans that would steal from a charity).

In <u>Good Works</u>, the authors touch on a few different types of criticisms that businesses may open themselves up to. One of which is,

"Lack of transparency about the amount, timing, or other aspects of a cause-related marketing program (e.g., stating that a nebulous portion of the proceeds from consumer purchases will be donated.)"

Raise your hand if you've ever been guilty of this? Don't worry, my hand is raised, too. For the last 3 years, I've announced that a portion of my book proceeds goes to Hearts Alive Village. In fact, my speaker's one-sheet even says that a portion of my speaking engagement fee will go to the rescue. I wasn't trying to be shifty, I just didn't realize that this could cause anyone to tilt their head to the side like a confused puppy.

The rule of thumb is that the customer must be able to "easily calculate the amount of the donation."

Instead of saying "a portion of the proceeds," I'll now say, "Two dollars from the sale of each book and 10% of my speaking fees goes to support Hearts Alive Village."

It seems like a small tweak, but Chansky explained the danger. Let's say that a business throws an event for a nonprofit. A "portion of the proceeds from the event" will go to the cause.

Now, the nonprofit has invited their supporters, put in time, energy, and possibly called in a few favors. The business has benefited from the use of the nonprofit's name and mission, and the event-goers attend the event (which they may not have otherwise) and spend money at the event (possibly more than they would have) because it's "going to a good cause."

In this unicorn-free scenario, the business could then turn around and say, "Well, the venue cost more than we expected, and the food ended up over budget, and we spent more on swag bags than we wanted... so we now have $6.24 to donate to the charity."

Ouch.

Let's just say that I now understand the need for checks and balances in this field, and I get it when people say that they don't trust that the money makes it to the charity. I get it. Transparency is important.

How do we fix the above situation and make it kosher for everyone involved? Change the wording to, "One hundred percent of ticket sales will go to the nonprofit," or "Twenty-five dollars from each ticket sold will benefit the cause." Want to keep your business even more in the clear? Have the ticket sales go DIRECTLY to the nonprofit. Do not pass Go, do not collect $200, and do not take the money into your account and then pass along a lump sum at the end of the event. Ask for a representative of the organization to work the door or set up a ticketing system that goes directly into the nonprofit's account.

"I'm Doing Good Things so my Business Will Do Well"

I would love to tell you that when you do good things, only good things come to you. Your business will skyrocket, money will literally grow on trees in your backyard, and you'll get a ride to work every day on the back of my unicorn friend.

Hell, I'd like to tell myself that. But, the reality is that you are still running a business.

Yanik Silver, author of Evolved Enterprise says, "You cannot simply believe if you are 'doing good' with your business that there's no need for a profitable and pragmatic business model. That's a recipe for quickly spiraling into anxiety and stress without the security of a strong financial foundation."

When my partner and I first announced the launch of the Cause Marketing Chamber of Commerce, we had a small group of dedicated members who attended every weekly meeting.

I was chatting with one of the women after a meeting and she said, "You're not going to be charging to be a member of this, are you?"

I had to take a deep breath and search my soul before I answered her.

If I were independently wealthy or married to a Persian Prince, I could devote every waking hour to volunteering... and I probably would (in between massages). However, as I am not independently wealthy, and my online dating has not yet yielded royalty, I need to keep a roof over my head and kibble in my dog's bowl.

Of course, I wasn't that much of a smart ass when I answered her.

"Yes, we will be charging. We are providing a service to businesses. Every chamber of commerce has a fee, and once we are up and running, and providing value to our members, we will as well. I spend a great deal of my time and energy volunteering to save animals. This is a business."

Yeah, she never came back. And, I haven't lost a single moment of sleep over it.

There are so many worthy causes out there that it's easy to get swept up trying to help everyone. The problem is, if you help everyone, if you spend all of your time donating your services, products, or money to nonprofits, you won't be able to stay in business. If you can't stay in business, you can't help anyone anymore.

In Marketing from the Heart, Peggy Linial refers to a keynote given by Gary Hirshberg, CEO of Stonyfield Farm (they make yogurt, soy and ice cream and are known for their support of environmental and organic farming causes).

> Hirshberg explains he once spoke to a group telling them about an available grant. One component, however, was that you must explain how that grant will impact the sales of yogurt in a positive way. When the audience was taken aback, Hirshberg went on to explain the philosophy saying, "If you cut the limbs off of an oak tree, there will be nothing left. However, if you simply drop acorns, eventually you will have many more oaks." By using this analogy, Hirshberg conveyed that while we all want to give, unless there is a return, we will be forced to cease our giving and then no one will benefit.

I'd refer back to <u>The Giving Tree</u> by Shel Silverstein here, but honestly, I don't want to be crying for the rest of the morning.

"But I Want Everyone to Like Me"

Did you suddenly become a jar of Nutella while reading the chapter? No? Then stop trying to get everyone to like you! (And I feel like now is a good time to mention that I recently found out that there are some horrific employee abuses in the hazelnut industry and the makers of Nutella are at the forefront of the behavior. [6]

Moving on.

After one of the many school shootings our country has experienced, Dick's Sporting Goods decided to take a stand against gun violence. CEO Edward W. Stack announced that the chain would no longer sell assault weapons, high-capacity magazines, or guns to customers under age 21. He also wrote a memo calling for common-sense gun reform and the passing of specific regulations.[7]

As previously mentioned, I live under a rock. So, most of my knowledge of the news comes from people reacting to it on Facebook. And, boy, did they react.

Facebook was in an uproar. The torches were lit and the pitchforks were polished. Second Amendment purists announced that they would never shop at Dick's Sporting Goods again.

And then there was the other side.

Facebook feeds were littered with individuals thanking Dick's for "protecting our kids" and "stepping in when the government wouldn't."

The market research company YouGove found that "public perception of Dick's Sporting Goods improved more than 40% following its announcement on gun sales. Based on aggregated visits at more than 700 Dick's stores across the country, Reveal Mobile found that overall foot traffic actually rose 3.7% in the days following its announcement."[8]

In November of that year, the company reported a 3.9% dip in sales, yet its profit margin had actually improved. Plus, other companies followed their lead.

After the announcement, Walmart announced that it, too, would stop selling guns and ammo to customers under the age of 21.[9]

When you take a stand on an issue or align yourself with a cause, you run the risk of alienating a portion of your customers. However, you'll also strengthen your position as a brand that cares about more than just making money.

Let the haters hate. You, my friend, are changing the world.

Section Two:

How to Incorporate Cause Marketing into Your Business

Chapter Five: Understand Your Why

"If you don't know where you are going, any road will get you there."

- Lewis Carroll

Set Your Goal

Whether you are starting a new Cause Marketing program, building a new business, writing a book, or getting married, I truly believe that the first question you must ask yourself is "Why?"

Approaching large undertakings with a sense of intentionality and purpose will not only make the journey quicker and easier, it will make the payoff more meaningful. Plus, you'll understand the driving force behind your decision which will keep you going on those days when you'd rather be doing ANYTHING other than working on your project.

Whereas most of this book is dedicated to making the world a better place, this question is all about you and your business. Feel free to be selfish right now.

Why do you want to start a Cause Marketing program?

Are you hoping to increase sales? Build brand awareness? Differentiate yourself from the competition?

Or do you just feel like life has been good to you and you'd like to spread some of that goodness around?

Understanding your Why, your goals, and ultimately, what you hope to get out of this experience, will affect the organization you collaborate with, the type of campaign you run, and how you judge your success at the end of it.

Chapter Six: Inventory Your Business

"I have nothing to offer but blood, toil, tears and sweat."

-Winston Churchill

Don't worry, you don't need to start counting widgets right now. When I talk about inventory, I'm actually referring to the different opportunities for cause-related assistance that your business can provide.

The authors of Global Cause Marketing, Hirsch and Gordon call this your T3: Time, Talent and Treasure.

Let's compare Cause Marketing to making a soup. Actually, let's make a chicken soup to serve the homeless.

What goes into a soup?

You'll need ingredients: Water, chicken stock, chicken, parsnips, celery, and parsley - also known as that green stuff I used to strain out as a kid.

Think that's all that's involved in making a chicken soup? Did you just take it for granted that you've got a pot and a heat source? Oh, and soup takes a long time to cook. Do you have a few hours to stand around and make sure the kitchen doesn't go up in flames?

I'm going to hop off that soup analogy before I have to stop writing to go cook. However, the process of making that soup is similar to creating an inventory of your business.

Here are some possibilities of what you can offer the nonprofit. We'll discuss the different types of Cause Marketing programs shortly, so for now, I'm just going to allude to them:

- Money
- Services
- Volunteer
- Products
- Physical location/ space
- "Real estate" boarding passes, bags, etc.
- Communication Channels

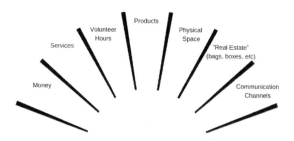

Business Inventory

Money

Can you afford to donate cash to an organization to support their programs and operating expenses. (If you just had a slight coronary, take a deep breath. We're going to get into operating expenses later.) This can be done through Point-of-Sale, Purchase-Triggered, Action-Triggered, and Donation-Triggered programs.

Services

What does your company actually do? Perhaps you own a mechanic shop and have a soft spot for Veterans. You could potentially partner with an organization that transports veterans to doctor's appointments and provides them with free auto maintenance and repair.

No matter what type of business you run (if it's large enough), you likely have an accountant, an IT person, and maybe an office manager. While you may not be able to spare them for a long period of time, you could give them a few hours off each month (paid) to help set up systems for a nonprofit and keep their organization running smoothly. Attorneys have understood the concept of Pro Bono for many years, as have creative professions like writers, graphic designers, videographers, etc. Now you can get involved in the same way.

Volunteer Hours

Nonprofits often struggle with finding enough labor. They have grand ideas to change the world but are doing it on a limited budget (more on that later), with little to no staff. Your business can participate in organized events like United Way's Day of Caring, or even better, dedicate a certain number of hours each month to volunteer with an organization.

Products

What do you sell and is it something a nonprofit could use? In addition to cause- and population-specific products like litter for an animal rescue or canned goods for a food pantry, nonprofits need everything that for-profit businesses need, like printer ink, cleaning supplies, and snacks for their employees/volunteers.

Physical location/ space

Do you have a building where nonprofits could host events? Extra warehouse space where you could store supplies for a nonprofit? How about a safe place for victims of natural disasters?

During Hurricane Harvey, Gallery Furniture Stores in Texas were closed for business so they could open their doors to evacuees (both humans and pets), giving them a safe place to escape the storm.[10]

"Real estate" boarding passes, bags, etc.

Don't forget the many physical items (not product) that your company uses. If you've got shopping bags or boxes, you could add a nonprofit's logo to bring awareness to your cause. Do you put package inserts in anything you sell; could you add on information about the nonprofit? The same goes for open space on tickets, boarding passes, receipts, uniforms, or vehicles that can be wrapped. The possibilities are endless.

Communication Channels

How do you communicate with your customers? Through email? Social Media? Physical mailings? Any communication channel becomes a good way to spread awareness for your message.

Now that you've determined why you want to help, and how you are able to help, it's time to select the beneficiary of your support.

Chapter Seven: Select Your Cause and Find a Nonprofit

I have an opportunity for you, Mr. or Ms. Business owner. This is very exciting, so I need you to sit down.

I'd like for you to come to work every day - no seriously, *every* day, like weekends too - for 8-12 hours each day.

I'd also like your entire staff to come to work for me.

I'm going to judge every penny you spend and question whether your methods are the most efficient. I mean, come on, do you really need a roof, office supplies, AND heat?

And here's the kicker... I'm not going to pay any of you. But don't worry, you are going to feel really good about what you do. In fact, you're going to be changing the world!

When your mortgage is due, don't worry about it. Just write, "I'm changing the world" on the invoice and mail it back.

When your kids need braces, just kindly explain to the orthodontist that you are changing the world. He'll zero out your balance immediately.

Food shopping? No worries. Just flash your handy dandy "I'm Changing the World" card and the supermarket will not only give you your groceries for free, but they'll also create a parade of gratitude to usher you towards your car.

Hold on just one second... do you not believe that this is going to happen? Are you not willing to work for free? Are you not willing to ask your staff to work for free? Do you have to keep a roof over your family's heads and food on the table? Do you need money to keep an office up and running and protected from the elements?

All sarcasm aside - can we now trash the antiquated BS thinking that:

1) Nonprofit employees should not make money; and
2) All of your donations and support must go to the programs and can't be used for operating expenses.

I remember the day that I received my cold slap to the face. I was horrified when I found out how much the CEO of our local food bank makes. I spouted out the common idea that, "Nonprofit executives don't need to make that much money." So a friend of mine directed me to a certain TED Talk. If you haven't watched Dan Pallotta's talk, please take 15 minutes and go look it up. I don't mind waiting. I actually haven't eaten breakfast yet, so I'll just grab a bite to eat.

https://www.ted.com/talks/dan_pallotta_the_way_we_t
hink_about_charity_is_dead_wrong?language=en

Welcome back!

Pretty hardcore, right? I watched that video and then sat
back feeling like a jerk for about 15 minutes before I
collected myself, sent an apology text to my friend, and
thanked her for opening my eyes.

Just in case you didn't take the time to watch it, I'll give
you the gist.

In order to operate and do their good work, nonprofits
need to spend money on operating expenses. If they
can't hire a CEO for a reasonable CEO salary, they can't
attract the best talent. And (this was my favorite part),
why does a CEO who sells violent video games to children
have the right to make more money than a CEO who is
curing children of malaria.

If you just sat back and let out a Keanu Reeves-esque,
"Whoah," then you've just been awakened.

He goes on to ask why we crucify the CEO that has
dedicated his life to the nonprofit and works for a
fraction of what he should be making, while we revere
the CEO who makes four times that and then donates
$100k to an organization or sits on its board?

I'll make one more point and then I'll hop down off this
soapbox.

I was at a fundraising seminar for animal rescuers a few weeks ago. When we introduced ourselves, one of the rescues stood up and proudly stated: "100% of our donations go to the animals. We don't take a salary and use all of our own money for the expenses."

This was truly a badge of honor for them.

I leaned forward in my chair and waited to see how the trainer would react. Thankfully, she pounced.

"It's wonderful that you've been financially able to support your own organization and not take a salary. However, this isn't something to be proud of or advertise."

I mentioned earlier that if a Persian Prince comes and whisks me off my feet, I'd be happy to fund a nonprofit. However, if the founders of a nonprofit are not independently wealthy, they are not going to survive.

As a business that is looking for a long-term collaboration with an organization that provides social value, if you hear a nonprofit tout their 0% overhead... run. That is not a sustainable, viable organization and, while you may provide some temporary assistance to the cause, they won't be around long enough to make a real difference.

Jumps down from soapbox

With that out of the way, how do you go about choosing a nonprofit to collaborate with?

What's Your Cause?

Selecting a nonprofit to collaborate with may be the most important decision you ever make (no pressure there).

How does one go about making this uber-important call? Well, there are two things to look at during this process:

1) What cause will you support?
2) What organization will you support?

Let's start with the cause. There are a few ways to select the societal issue that you'll help eradicate:

Heart Alignment

What do you care about? What population tugs at your heartstrings? What situation is currently making your blood boil?

Was your father a veteran? Did your grandmother die of breast cancer? When you were a child, do you remember the embarrassment of being called to the office to pick up your "weekend bag of food?"

When I think about animals being mistreated, abused, or killed due to lack of space... I want to start throat-punching people. I'm not going to say that I don't care about helping the homeless, children, Veterans, or anyone else - however, my heart belongs to animals. And that's okay. You can't fix every problem. Pick one for now and when you make your billions, you can support everyone.

If you are a solopreneur, there's only one person you need to convince... you. However, if you work with a team, there may be more opinions to take into consideration. There are two sides to this coin. The first is the glass-half-full side: when your team has a say in something, they are more invested in the outcome. The second side is the glass-half-empty side: everyone has a different opinion and you might alienate some of your staff by giving everyone voting rights. Whichever world view you subscribe to, whether you involve your employees is up to you.

Industry Alignment

What makes sense with your industry? If you are a restaurant, it would make sense to align with a hunger charity because you have similar missions (feeding people, if that was not glaringly obvious). If you are a realtor, you may support an organization that provides housing for low-income individuals. Or you may have walked into multiple foreclosed homes where the family pet was left behind, so now you want to help animals.

Of course, there's another side to this. What about collaborations that make NO sense and could damage the reputation of the nonprofit or the business?

Let me throw out a few examples:

What if a cigarette company decided to raise money for hungry children? Granted, intentions may be pure, but should cigarettes and children really be mentioned in the same conversation? Are there any natural connections between the two? Nope. Does a nonprofit that feeds children want to be associated with a dangerous industry that's been accused of marketing to kids? Probably not. It reminds me of a Chris Rock movie I watched years ago. In Head of State, he was trying to raise funds for his campaign and came across an alcohol company that was packaging their products in baby bottles... all while saying they didn't support underage drinking. Fail.

Another failed collaboration: Every single book I've read on the topic has brought up the KFC and Susan G. Komen snafu. KFC created a "Buckets for the Cure" promotion with a pink-branded website with stories of survivors and facts about the disease. They designed special pink buckets and pledged to donate 50 cents from the sale of each one of these buckets to support the fight against breast cancer. Do you see the problem? Apparently using unhealthy, fried, potentially cancer-causing food to raise money for breast-cancer research is not a great idea. I have to imagine that was a plan concocted after one too many drinks at the bar. To be fair, they raised about $4 million dollars for the organization. Worth the fallout? You decide.

You CAN collaborate with anyone you want (who's willing), but you need to consider the consequences.

You can also stand for anything you want... but you might want to think the idea through fully before getting started. Take Burger King's most recent train wreck – I mean Cause Marketing campaign. #Feelyourway appears to be a combination of mental health awareness, bizarre product launch (Unhappy Meals), and bashing McDonalds.

The internet backlash was pretty severe. From people who used to work at Burger King and didn't feel their emotional wellbeing was supported, to those who don't feel fat-laden foods can help improve mood, most people agreed the fast-food chain had gone too far.

Watching the video, I'm also concerned about placing daily frustrations (like being angry at your boss) in the same category as clinical depression. I've experienced both and they are light years apart.

Did Burger King have the right to attach their brand to mental-health awareness[11]? Yes. But is there another cause that would've been better suited? Probably.

Customer Alignment

In Cause Marketing for Dummies, Waters and MacDonald suggest that you "Determine whether the cause's donors fit the demographics of your company's customers and prospects."

Makes sense, right? If part of your Why is to increase brand awareness and sales, aligning with a nonprofit that is actually in front of your potential customers makes good sense.

The flip side: Do you want to take a stand against your potential customers? Think back to the example I gave earlier about Dick's Sporting Goods. They took a very brazen stance on gun control and, in doing so, alienated potential customers and vendors who thought otherwise. It worked out okay for them, but if you're going to stand up for something, make sure you're willing to lose some followers. Causes can be very polarizing.

Follow the Donation Requests

If you've been in business for more than ten minutes, you've likely been bombarded with requests for donations. Local nonprofits, church groups, softball teams, they all need help.

However, do you have a product that lends itself to a certain cause?

I recently spoke to Jake Neeley with the Malouf Foundation. Malouf Sleep has been in business for approximately 16 years making sheets, pillows, mattress protectors, and more. They had a wide variety of nonprofits asking for donations, many of which were domestic violence shelters and foster care facilities that were looking to provide a comfortable night's sleep to people while helping to get them back on their feet.

The more Malouf donated and worked with the organizations, the more they learned about the problems such organizations were facing. The cause struck a chord.

For purposes of transparency and ease of donating, they decided to start their own foundation to help stop human trafficking and prevent the exploitation of children. Learn more at https://malouffoundation.org/.

I know we already talked about the benefits of standing for a cause in an earlier chapter, but it's worth mentioning that Malouf's charitable involvement has become so ingrained in their culture that they attract top talent who are more interested in making a difference, than in making a dollar. In fact, one of Jake's coworkers left a lot of money on the table during a counteroffer, because he believed so strongly in what the company stands for. We'll discuss the different ways in which the Malouf Foundation is helping, in a later chapter.

Do you have a few causes in mind? Make a list of the top three or four social issues that you care about. Once you've done that, we can discuss whether or not size matters.

Size of the nonprofit, of course!

Perhaps you subscribe to the school of thought that bigger is always better. From a marketing perspective, it makes sense. Do you want to collaborate with an organization that has branches in all 50 states and has a brand name recognizable to even the most agoraphobic hermit?

That sounds like a great plan!

There's just one problem. You are a small business. You are not Pepsi, Microsoft, or Macy's. The amount of money that you will be able to generate for these large nonprofits is a minuscule, practically insignificant spot on their annual budget.

Are you supporting a good cause? For sure. Are you truly making a difference... probably not.

Your other option is focusing your efforts on a small, local nonprofit whose financial situation and social impact could be greatly improved thanks to your help.

Want some science to back that up? In Cause Marketing for Dummies, the authors said, "Consumers want companies to act locally. This point is critical for local causes and businesses that may feel that Cause Marketing is only for bigger charities and companies.

Nearly half of the respondents to the 2017 Cone study said a company should focus on issues that impact local communities. And 91 percent said that companies should support an issue in the communities where they do business."

Let's hop back to that big charity for a moment. I don't want to throw anyone under the bus, so I'll just call it Big

National Charity (BNC). You, Bob the small-town Realtor, want to support Big National Charity. You call them up looking to speak to their marketing department. Maybe you get through, maybe you get the runaround. Either way, you decide to move forward because you really want to help them.

Do you think that BNC is going to put effort into getting press coverage for you? Nope. Your contribution is not worth the effort. You'll probably get a thank-you letter. Maybe it will be handwritten. Maybe not.

However, when you partner with Tiny Local Charity (TLC - and I totally didn't do that on purpose), they are going to be so much more grateful. Your support may be the difference between lives lost or saved. Your support may allow them to start a new program or finally have the manpower they need to make a real difference.

Are they going to try and get media coverage for you... absolutely. Are they going to share your support with their followers and donors... absolutely. Are they going to do everything in their power (more about this in the nonprofit section) to direct customers your way? Yup. They have a vested interest.

In The Collaboration Challenge, author Austin says, "One of the powerful characteristics of collaboration is that it is not scale-dependent. That is, you don't have to be big to enter into a meaningful relationship with a nonprofit organization. Small can be beautiful."

Obviously, I agree. I just want to add to that the small charities can be beautiful, too. And collaborating with an organization that's approximately the same size, and that operates in the same community as you do business (even if they don't have brand recognition across the country), is more powerful than choosing a huge organization.

Find Organizations That Fit the Bill

You've narrowed down your possibilities. You've determined what cause you'd like to support and you've decided to support a small, local charity (if you haven't, go read that last section again until you're convinced).

Now it's time to identify the specific nonprofit you'd like to work with.

 How?

There are a few ways. The least enjoyable (in my opinion) is to search the IRS database. If you'd like to sort through a bazillion or so organizations, please go here: https://www.irs.gov/charities-nonprofits/tax- exempt-organization-search-bulk-data-downloads

Not appealing? Why don't you just ask around?

Two months ago, I was tagged in a post on Facebook. A new poop-scooping company called Oh Crap posed a question to their followers:

"We are looking to donate a portion of our proceeds to an animal rescue here in town. Who knows a good one?"

Within 10 minutes, their feed was full of potential animal rescues to work with. I just happened to be checking Facebook moments after I was tagged and I responded immediately with "Hearts Alive Village! You definitely want to work with us," and a link to our website.

Within moments, five people had chimed in and confirmed that we were indeed awesome; which will segue nicely into our next section.

There are probably listings in your community that showcase all of the different nonprofits. However, it's just as easy to ask for suggestions from your supporters - plus, you have the added bonus of letting them know you'll be supporting a nonprofit before you even start.

Do Your Due Diligence

My world of unicorns was already destroyed regarding businesses and honesty... let's go ahead and shatter the nonprofit side, too.

Not all nonprofits are created equal.

Hopefully, you took the time to watch Dan Pallotta's TEDtalk that I posted earlier. If you did, you'll understand why I'm not going to bash any charities for paying their employees, keeping the heat on in the building, or even using donation money for advertising.

That all being said, there are some dishonest charities out there. There are Executive Directors who siphon money out of the organization and employees who mistreat whatever population it is they're supposed to be caring for. As a business, you don't want to get caught up with a bad seed. Not only will you not make a difference in the social cause you've chosen, but you'll also potentially damage your reputation.

"It takes 20 years to build a reputation and five minutes to ruin it." - Warren Buffett

That's part of the brilliance of Oh Crap's method. They not only got the names of potential rescues, they learned about the reputations these rescues have in the community.

People are happy to tell you when they like an organization and even happier to tell you when they don't.

You'll also want to look at the board. Who is serving on their board? Do you know anyone there or could you be connected to someone to get the inside scoop?

There are also outside resources that you can utilize to find nonprofits on the up and up. You can review sites such as:

- BBB Wise Giving Alliance reviews 501c3s
- AIP Charity Rating Guide
- Charitywatch.org

Please keep in mind when you review these sites that not everyone has the enlightened concept of nonprofit spending that you now have. One more time... did you watch the TEDtalk? Seriously, what are you waiting for?

Talk to the Nonprofit

Before you go brandishing another organization's logo around like a mystical marketing weapon, you really ought to talk to them first.

Remember how I mentioned that not every business and nonprofit alliance is a match made in heaven? While every nonprofit needs money, they may not want yours. Sound harsh? Sorry. Nonprofits have to protect their reputation, too.

If you "borrow" a nonprofit's brand without asking... that's Non-consensual Collaborating (just made that up, but I'm going to run with it.)

Always ask permission. In fact...

Make it Legal

Once again, I can't imagine that anyone would say they're going to do something for a nonprofit and then not, but it happens. Be clear about exactly what this collaboration will entail upfront so that there are no misunderstandings. Here is a sample contract that you can use: https://engageforgood.com/cause- marketing-101-for-nonprofits/

Outlining everything upfront will protect against any confusion or damaged relationships later on.

Chapter Eight: Choose Your Strategy

You now know what Cause Marketing is. You're convinced that it's the best thing since sliced bread. You've chosen your cause, connected with your nonprofit partner, and you are ready to...

What? How exactly does one do Cause Marketing?

Now, we're getting into the meat and potatoes of Cause Marketing (or the tofu and greens for my vegan friends).

We're going to start out with some traditional Cause Marketing strategies and then look at some of the newer, different ways that you can get involved with a nonprofit. I'll use some national examples that you've probably heard of; but, since this book is really focused on helping out the small-business owner, I've interviewed a few local businesses that engage in Cause Marketing. This way, you can see how people just like you have gotten involved with nonprofits.

Put your scuba suits on, we're diving in!

Traditional Cause Marketing is very transactional in nature. The two most common types of campaigns are Point of Sale (pinups) and Action Triggered.

Point of Sale

You've likely been in the checkout line at your local supermarket and noticed cutouts decorating the register.

They're either sneakers or hot air balloons, maybe even a shamrock. You see that people's names are written on these shapes. When you get to the cashier, she asks you if you'd like to donate $1 to a specific charity to support a cause. You probably agree (because it's only $1) and the total is added to your bill while you add your name to a shape.

These point-of-sale campaigns generally last for two to four weeks. Why?

A few years ago, I worked as a greeter at conventions (you do what you gotta do when you're building a business). I would start out the day bright and fresh, smiling, welcoming everyone who walked through the doors and clearly articulating directions to the different ballrooms. But there's only so many times you can say, "Welcome to CES! The keynote will be held on the second floor of the convention space. Just head down that corridor, up to the second floor, and make a right. Have a great day!" By the end of the day, I was reduced to pointing and unintelligible grunting. I was exhausted.

Fatigue affects point-of-sale campaigns, as well. Both on the part of the customer who is tired of being asked every time they come to the store, and also, on the part of the cashier who has to repeat the same line every three minutes.

It gets old, so you keep it short.

This is considered an Active point-of-sale campaign. There are also Passive campaigns where the donation request is made electronically through the payment system. If you've ever purchased anything at PetSmart, you've probably seen the "Would you like to donate $1 to support homeless animals?" question at the credit card reader.

Does it work? Yes? As good as an Active campaign? Not really.

If you have a brick-and-mortar space that you'd like to use for a point-of-sale campaign, make sure to coordinate with the nonprofit. Ask if a representative will come in to talk to your employees about what their organization does and how to make the ask. Even better, give your employees time to go tour the nonprofit's facility (if they have one) or to volunteer with the charity so they can build an emotional connection with the cause.

Provide t-shirts for your employees to volunteer in and to work in. That way, when repeat customers notice that something is different, they can ask about the details of the collaboration even before they're asked to donate at the register.

You can also create co-branded materials with your logo and all of the nonprofit's info to hand out with each donation. This way, you're not only raising money, but you're also raising awareness. And, oh yeah... look, your information is on there, too.

Wendy's used a similar technique with those Frosty coupons. They not only gave customers the opportunity to donate (and be the hero), they also gave them an incentive to do so, and to return to the restaurant.

Don't have a brick and mortar? If you sell online, you can still create a point-of-sale program at checkout. When customers head to their shopping cart, add a page asking if they'd like to donate to the charity you've chosen. Even better, match whatever donation they're willing to give.

Action Triggered

Remember learning logic back in high school math? If (you do something) then (something happens). Action-triggered donations are the same thing.

Buy One, Give One: If you purchase a product, a product will be donated to someone in need.

The most famous example of this is TOMS shoes, which donates a pair of shoes to a child for every pair sold.

One of my personal favorite examples is Passion Planner. A few years ago, I was in the market for a new paper calendar (I'm analog and proud of it). I asked a friend/productivity specialist which one she recommended; she sent me to a blog she'd recently written reviewing six different planners.

The first one on the list was the Passion Planner. I went over to their website and immediately saw that for every planner sold, a planner is donated to someone in need, and a percentage of the profit is donated to a charity.

Were there other planners on her list? Yes. Were they just as good, if not better, than the one I chose? No idea. All I know is that even though the donated planners weren't going to animals — and they do have very active social schedules — I believed in what the company was doing and I wanted to support it. I'm on my fourth planner and I don't even bother shopping anymore. The only decision I have to make is what color planner I want. Each color supports a different nonprofit, so you have the option to choose based on color or on who you'd like to support. My planner this year supported the Leukemia and Lymphoma Society.

As soon as I get the email that the next year's planner is available, I order it. How's that for brand loyalty?

In Evolved Enterprise, Silver talks about Bombas Socks. The company got started when David Heath and Randy Goldberg discovered that socks were the #1 requested item at homeless shelters. They decided to create a better sock, and for every pair purchased, they'd donate a pair to someone in need. In just 1.5 years, they surpassed their goal of donating 1 million pairs.

If you'd like to learn more about this type of giving model and find potential causes to support, visit www.B1G1.com.

A purchase can trigger a donation of the same product, of money, or even of in-kind services. And sometimes, you don't have to make a purchase.

A few years ago, I was working a booth for the rescue at a networking event. A man came up to me and asked what we were all about. I did my spiel and he immediately said he wanted to help.

I generally like to believe the best of people; however, every time I'm at a networking event, at least 10 people tell me they want to help. Guess how many of those usually pan out?

If you said "0" you'd be right.

That's why I was surprised when he called me a few days later. He'd done more research on Hearts Alive and now he was really excited to get involved.

"I've been looking for a charity to support for two years now. None of them seemed right until I spoke to you."

Cool.

Rob Martinez is an insurance agent for Liberty Mutual. They've got a Quote for Donation program whereby, every time you get a car or home insurance quote, $5 or $10 is donated to the charity.

We've been working with Rob for almost three years now. He's raised around $3k for us and saved some of our supporters money on their insurance. He has sponsored our events, raised awareness for our cause, and at our last big event, he took our founder aside and said, "You guys have pretty much built my business." That is the win-win nature of Cause Marketing.

Let's take a look at some less-traditional Cause-Marketing or collaboration strategies.

Share Real Estate

In addition to PetSmart's passive point-of-sale donation program, they also offer space to local rescues. Have you ever walked through the store and seen the cutest kitten or most adorable pooch vying for your attention? This is because PetSmart decided not to sell dogs and cats (good choice), and instead, to donate space for adoption events.

The authors of Good Works said,

> The adoption centers generate store traffic on a daily basis from consumers looking for a pet to add to their families. Publicity around national and community adoption events in individual stores, often supported by corporate sponsors, drives traffic even higher. In 2010, more than 403,000 pets were adopted in PetSmart Stores.

And it's not just the big, chain pet stores that are getting involved.

Gena Bunim has owned At Your Service Pet Supplies, a Henderson, Nevada-based pet-supply store/grooming and self-wash business, since 2008. Last year, she opened her second location in Las Vegas.

The store sells pet supplies, including better nutrition for companion animals like dogs, cats, birds, and critters. Since day one, Gena has understood the value of working with nonprofits. "I saw all of these rescue groups with great intentions. They just needed a space to adopt out animals."

The store provides a location for local rescue groups to host adoption events. She also has donation bins at the counter and a Round-Up for Rescue program at the register. Customers are asked if they'd like to round up their order and the money goes into a pool. At the end of the month, the money is divided up between the rescues that hosted adoption events that month.

Throughout the year, the stores will also host events like self-wash or animal-care fundraisers. Gena said, "The local parrot rescue came in to do nail trimmings and there was a line out the door. Customers were happy to pay $35 to the rescue and enjoyed seeing all of the other birds while they waited. The rescue offered to split the money with the store but I refused. 'Look how many customers you brought in!'"

Not only are customers happy to come in for events, but they keep coming back. Foot traffic increases with each adoption event and when someone adopts a pet at her store, they usually become a customer for life. It's exciting for the staff to see the animal find a forever family and then return every few weeks. "We love to see how they're doing!"

Increased sales and brand loyalty aren't the only benefits Gena has seen in her business. With so many animal rescues coming through, they've shared their wealth of knowledge with her staff.

For more information on At Your Service Pet Supplies, visit https://www.atyourservicepetsupplies.com/

Cause Promotion

According to Kotler, Hessekiel, and Lee,

> Cause promotion leverages corporate funds, in-kind contributions, or other resources to increase awareness and concern about a social cause or to support fundraising, participation, or volunteer recruitment for a cause. Well-conceived and executed cause promotions can improve attitudes toward a company; generate consumer traffic, sales, and increased loyalty; and motivate employees and trade partners. (Good Works)

Remember, sometimes in business we need to play the long game. While this type of marketing can produce a few immediate sales, it's more effective for brand and relationship building.

In Good Works, the authors discuss the following communication objectives of Cause Promotion:

- Building awareness and concern for the cause - your customers may not even be aware of the social issues in their own backyard. You can educate your audience with the stories of the people or animals affected by this problem.
- Persuading people to find out more about the cause - now that they're aware of the problem, point them to an organization that's working to find the solution.
- Persuading people to donate their time - that poop-scooping company I mentioned earlier doesn't just want to help us with financial support, they want to create a community of people who volunteer their time at our adoption center and our events.
- Persuading people to donate money - some companies have a link on their website that allows you to donate directly to the charity.
- Persuading people to donate non-monetary resources - while charities always need money, they also need stuff like office supplies, cleaning supplies, gas cards, canned food, clothing, etc.
- Persuading people to get involved - does the charity have an upcoming event that people

can participate in? How about a petition that they'll bring before a governing body?

Thank You or Follow Up

Every good salesperson knows that the relationship is not over once the sale has closed. There's always the possibility of repeat business and referrals.

The way that you handle the 'thank you' at the end of the transaction can also show your support of a specific cause.

Two years ago, I was hired to tour the luxury home listings throughout Las Vegas with nine of the top realtors in the country and then write an article for a magazine. We loaded ourselves into a luxury bus and spent the time between homes discussing their businesses and uncovering what made their service stand out above others.

My favorite one was the realtor who said that he'd find out what cause or specific charity a client supported and, instead of giving them a bottle of wine to say thank you, he'd make a donation in their name.

Sidenote: Want to hear something cool? About an hour after I wrote that last paragraph up there about that generous real estate agent, I got a phone call from a fellow board member (and a good friend) at the rescue. There's another real estate agent in town who has decided to donate a portion of each of his closings to local charities. He chose one children's charity and us.

He'd like us to send a letter to his clients notifying them of the donation made in their name. Yeah... we can do that.

Hardcore Helpers

In <u>Evolved Enterprise</u>, Silver talks about companies that are "All In" and give away all of their profits to organizations that are aligned with the company's values. Newman's Own is a great example that's been in the public eye for years. If you'd like to learn more about their business model of 100% of profit to charity (after regular expenses), check them out here: https://www.newmansown.com/100-percent-profits-to-charity/

However, reading this book was the first time I'd heard about Greyston Bakery. I had a (good) visceral reaction when I read their philosophy: "We don't hire people to bake brownies, we bake brownies to hire people." I literally got goosebumps.

The bakery was founded in 1982 based on the Buddhist tenets of non-judgment and loving action. The company has trademarked their Open Hiring (TM) model, which allows them to hire anyone willing to work. This includes people of all colors, faiths, and sexual orientations; those who served time in prison; those living in poverty; even refugees.

All profits from the company go to the Greyston Foundation, which supports a wide variety of causes, including workforce development for "hard-to-employ" populations; the Maitri Center for individuals living with HIV/AIDS; a childcare center and after-school programs; affordable housing services for homeless, low-income, and/or single-parent families; and more.

If that isn't enough, they are the exclusive global brownie supplier for Ben & Jerry's ice cream. Be still my heart.

Learn more at greyston.com, and please excuse me while I track down someone to join me for ice cream tonight.

Employee Support

If one of your main goals of working with a cause is to get your employees more invested, or even to attract better employees, consider how they can be involved. Many companies offer paid time off to volunteer. VTO (Volunteer time off) is becoming more and more common. According to the 2018 Employee Benefits Report[12], approximately one in four companies and nonprofits in the U.S. now offer VTO to their employees. This is up from 15% of employers in 2009.

Taking this idea even further, Apple not only pays its employees to volunteer, but also pays the nonprofit for the time employees spend there.[13] When Bert "Tito" Beveridge founded his vodka company, he couldn't afford to advertise or market his product. His solution? He gave it away to local nonprofits for their fundraising events. Philanthropy remains a part of the culture at Tito's and the brand identifies itself as a charity company that, "just happens to sell vodka on the side."

Tito's also encourages all employees to support a cause close to their heart through the use of a "joy budget," which provides vodka to charities of their choice. The company has now expanded their charity program to include an annual "pot of gold" — money employees can use to support their chosen nonprofit.[14]

A Note About B-Corps

It's impossible to research Cause Marketing or any type of conscious capitalism without coming across the term B-Corp.

A B-Corp, or Benefit Corporation, is NOT a nonprofit. This type of entity is still a for-profit organization and has NO tax-exempt status. According to attorney Gina Bongiovi, "The benefit of a B-Corp is that it allows a for-profit company to subordinate its fiduciary duty to turn a profit to a larger, more 'beneficial' goal."

Do you need this in non-lawyer speak? Don't be embarrassed, I bought her coffee so she'd dumb this down for me.

Basically, when you've got a corporation, you are responsible to your shareholders to operate in their best interests (and most shareholders believe that means pursuing profit). With a B-Corp, those duties are slightly

lessened so that you can focus on improving the world —
even if it means sacrificing a profit.

If you choose to set up a B-Corp, you will have oodles of
extra paperwork to file; you will have to state your
"cause" upfront; and, you'll have to stick with it. You'll
also be under a bunch of scrutiny.

Want more information? Check out this article:
https://bongiovilaw.com/2014/01/benefit-corporations/
and then contact an attorney who specializes in this type
of law.

Back to Cause Marketing!

The sky is the limit when it comes to what kind of
campaign you can run. Take your assets, the nonprofit's
needs, and your goals into account, and then get
creative!

Jake at Malouf suggests asking the question, "How can I
make a difference for this cause?"

As you work with a nonprofit, you're likely to notice
other areas that you can support them in. For example,
many of the nonprofits Malouf worked with sold stickers
and other merchandise to raise money. Well, Malouf has
warehouses all around the U.S. to ship their products. It
was a natural fit to offer shipping services for the
nonprofit's products.

Then, the more they learned about law enforcement's involvement in protecting children from criminals online, the more Malouf realized that law enforcement was lacking the staff to deal with the problem. The solution?

Malouf's software engineers are currently working to create AI bots that act as vulnerable children online and identify these criminals before they can hurt anyone.

The potential contributions may not be obvious when you first agree to work with a cause. However, if you keep your eyes open, you may see more opportunities than you could possibly imagine.

When I was in high school, "The Crow" was my favorite movie. I literally watched it every day for a full year. I also may or may not have dated a guy for nine months because he dressed up as the character for Halloween. But that's beside the point.

At the end of the video, there was an interview with Brandon Lee. In it, he explained how amazing it was portraying a man who had come back from the dead because no one knew how he was supposed to act.

While Cause Marketing has been around for many years now, and there are a number of businesses that incorporate it, the market is nowhere near saturated and the official rules are still being written. Allow your desire to improve the world guide your decisions, and you'll make good ones.

Chapter Nine: Outline Your Cause-Marketing or Promotion Campaign Plan

So far, we've been discussing how to select your cause, collaborate with the right nonprofit, and select the type of campaign you'll carry out. The following chapters will help you put all of this together and create a clear plan that you can share with everyone involved and use as a guidepost for your endeavor.

Why do I need a plan?

I know you just want to make a difference. So why can't you just jump in and get started?

Herein lays the difference between Cause Marketing and regular ol' donations. If you want to donate to a charity or 37 charities, go for it! Get out your checkbook and start firing off moola to groups doing good work. There's nothing wrong with that.

But what we're talking about here is more than just writing checks. I'm going to throw some corporate buzzwords your way, so bear with me for a moment.

You are creating a strategic collaboration with a nonprofit or cause that will enable you to build your business while making an impact on the community.

Corporate buzzwords out of the way... you need a plan or your actions will be all willy-nilly and not do the good you want to do.

Got it?

Ideally, a Cause-Marketing Plan will be 2-3 pages and will answer the following questions:

1. Who are you trying to reach? Who is your ideal customer?
2. What is your cause and why are you supporting it? (We'll talk about crafting your story in a bit.)
3. What nonprofit have you decided to work with?
4. What do you want the customer to do? Do you want them to volunteer? Donate money? Purchase a product so you can donate money?
5. What does your customer get out of helping? Remember that you should always position your marketing copy through the What's In It For Me or WIIFM attitude (we'll discuss that in a bit).
6. Where and how will you reach your audience? This should include what you take on, as well as what the nonprofit plans to do. We'll discuss Marketing and Public Relations shortly.
7. What will your marketing look like? Are you going for humorous or serious? The tone of a campaign can influence its success. You'll need

to take your target audience into account, as well as the cause itself.

8. What are your goals for this promotion or collaboration? What will a "successful" campaign look like? How will you measure it?

Once this document has been created, make sure that everyone involved in the campaign has the opportunity to review it. The more in sync your team is with the overall goal, the better you'll fair.

Chapter Ten: Craft Your Story

"The giving component of TOMS makes our shoes more than a product. They're a part of a story, a mission, and a movement anyone can join."

- Blake Mycoskie

This chapter is special because this is where my business and my life all came together. My journey to professional speaker hasn't been a direct route.

I remember sitting in my National Speaker's Association Academy class wracking my brain for my "expertise." You see, when you go into the speaking world, it's made quite clear that you are not a professional speaker... you are an expert.

Fantastic! Unless, of course, you are a Jane of All Trades like I am. I've worked in almost every industry, have a random degree that no one knows what to do with, my hobbies are varied, and I'm always working on enough projects to make even Oprah dizzy.

Then we had a guest speaker at the monthly meeting - branding genius Dick Bruso. He asked the most powerful question I've ever been asked. "If you only had ten minutes to speak to thousands of people, and then you could never speak again, what would you say?"

I didn't have to think for more than a second, "When you help others, you help yourself."

After my divorce, my depression, and years of trying to find my place in this world, that was the number one thing that I'd learned. I wanted to shout it from the rooftops!

Unfortunately, I was quickly informed that no one was going to pay for me to tell them to volunteer.

Ouch.

I'll make a long story short now. I went down a path that I didn't want to go down. I decided I could help other people struggling with depression and challenges. I wrote my first book, <u>Surviving to Thriving: How to Overcome Setbacks and Rock Your Life</u>. I'm glad I did. No matter how much I love my other books, that will always be my favorite. Every time someone approaches me and says my book helped them; it becomes my favorite all over again.

I also decided I'd be a resilience coach. I forgot that I wanted to keynote and began looking for one-on-one clients whom I could coach through difficult times.

Unfortunately, it wasn't where my heart was.

The day that storytelling popped into my head, I was sitting in a starlight meditation session at a writing retreat. I rarely stop moving, talking, or thinking, so sitting still in silence for 20 minutes was quite the stretch. However, something allowed me to relax into the soft grass and quiet my mind.

"Once upon a bottom line."

It was like some sort of divine download. I saw the words before my eyes and questioned what they could possibly mean. "Once upon" seemed like storytelling, "bottom line" was obviously business. Hmm. It just so happened that I'd written three novels to date... and oh yeah, I'd been writing website content and marketing materials for businesses for a few years at that point.

Maybe, I was an expert in storytelling for business.

Skeptical as always, and tired of chasing career squirrels, I asked for a sign. Just twenty minutes later, we finished up the meditation and I headed into the main lobby to use the potty. Sitting on the promotional table was a card that said:

Share Your Story to Help Others

Sedona Mago Retreat values your retreat experience. Your testimonial is a wonderful tool for others to make an informed decision. Please take a moment and tell your story at...

I went home and immediately began researching how to teach storytelling, wrote my book, and now offer workshops and keynotes.

Where am I going with all of this? I told you this story for two reasons:

1) To show (rather than tell) you what an Origin story looks like. Borrowed from the world of comic books, origin stories give us insight into someone and allow us to understand where they are coming from and why they do what they do. This is one of the essential stories that you must have in your business arsenal.
2) To introduce the third story I believe you need to have in that arsenal (and what differentiates me from other storytelling speakers)... the Cause Marketing story. This goes beyond why you do what you do to examine why you support what you support.

In Chapter One, I actually told you my Cause Marketing story, do you remember it?

Divorce - depression - bathroom floor - stepmom says to go help someone else - I found animal rescue... remember?

Animals helped save my life and I will spend the rest of mine saving theirs.

When you meet me, you'll hear this story in one fashion or another, probably before you even know what I do for a living. Yes, it differentiates me from other writers and storytellers (and there are a lot of us), but more importantly, it helps me connect with people on a human level.

Ever wonder why TOMS does what it does? Here's an excerpt from Blake's bio on their website:

> While traveling in Argentina in 2006, Blake witnessed the hardships faced by children growing up without shoes. His solution to the problem was simple, yet revolutionary: to create a for-profit business that helped such children, but that was sustainable and not reliant on donations. Blake's vision soon turned into the simple business idea that provided a powerful foundation for TOMS. (https://www.toms.com/blakes-bio)

In Start Something that Matters, there's a more detailed, emotional description of the change he underwent on that trip. But in a nutshell, that's his Cause Marketing story.

Whether you grew up poor, lost a loved one to a certain disease, found solace in nature, or found peace in 4 paws and a snout, you have a story to share with the world.

When you share this Cause Marketing story, your business's collaboration with a nonprofit and your support of a cause become more than just a marketing ploy, it becomes an emotional connection that your existing and potential customers can feel.

Did you just shake your head and mumble, "But I'm not a storyteller."?

Sure, you are. In fact, not only have you been conditioned since birth to respond to story, if you've ever done anything wrong as a child, and then blamed it on a sibling or the poor family dog... you are a storyteller.

Now, I wrote a whole book about this and if you want to learn the ins and outs of storytelling, I suggest you buy Once Upon a Bottom Line: Harnessing the Power of Storytelling in Sales. You can download the first chapter for free at www.onceuponabottomline.com.

But you bought this book... so I'll give you some basic storytelling goodness.

Here's what you need to tell a story. (I'll be referring back to mine for convenience.)

1) A purpose. If you are telling a story purely for entertainment, you can skip this one. If you are telling a story to a potential customer, you better have a reason for telling it — or the ability to give them the last 20 minutes of their life back.

The purpose of my Cause Marketing story is that I want you to care about animal rescue and do business with me.

2) Life as it was. Your audience needs someone to care about (a character), a setting (so they can picture the scene), and just enough backstory to understand the situation.

110

The character was me, the setting was my parent's bathroom, and my backstory was a horrendous divorce.

3) Boot-to-Butt Moment. Something happens to disturb the character's peaceful existence. Life is forever changed.

Depending on how much of the story I share, the Boot-to-Butt moment could be when my husband was arrested or when I hit my rock bottom on the bathroom floor.

4) Goal. What does your character want?

I wanted to get up, get on with my life, and shake off the clinical depression.

5) Conflict. What's standing in the way of that goal?

Clinical depression.

6) Attempts. What has the character tried to reach their goal?

I tried therapy, personal-development books, antidepressants, and A LOT of ice cream.

7) Solution. How do they eventually reach their goal?

Animal Rescue!!!!!

8) Life As it is Now. Some stories end before the "denouement" — that's the official term — however, we

humans like closure. What does life look like now that the character has been through this mess?

I'm living happily and rescuing fuzzbutts.

9) Call to Action (CTA). Remember in # 1 where I said you don't need a purpose for a purely entertainment story? Same thing goes for a CTA. However, if you'd like your audience to purchase a product, make a donation, sign with you as a client, or take any other steps, you need to actually ask them.

This could be something like, "Animals saved my life and I'll spend the rest of mine saving theirs. When you hire me as a speaker or consultant, more animals get saved. Will you hire me?"

That's a bit clunky, but you get the gist of it.

That's your down and dirty lesson on storytelling. Always remember those elements and the most important aspect of storytelling: Without emotion in your story, you'll miss out on the connection with your audience.

> Stop trying to promote your brand. Instead, imagine what happens if your brand stands for something. If your brand has a strong authentic cause at its core then your cause becomes your content. Get it right and what will happen next is that your own customer — your tribe — will take up your story themselves. They'll start promoting

your stories and with your stories, your brand. (Path to Purpose)

Chapter Eleven: PR and Marketing

Yes, this whole book is about marketing, but if you don't let the world know what you're doing, the world won't know what you're doing. Oh yeah, that's all sorts of tweetable, isn't it?

Collaborating with a cause will help you gain attention and favor, but you still have to put yourself out there. Imagine the woman who gets all dolled up. She does her hair, her makeup, puts on a beautiful dress, and then sits on the couch and watches reruns of "The Office." She's probably not going to meet anyone tonight, never mind get asked out on a date. However, if she dresses up and then GOES OUT, she might just meet the man of her dreams.

Throughout this book, you've been putting on your makeup and doing your hair. Now, it's time to get in the car and head to the bar, or the club, or wherever it is that single people meet each other these days. Seriously, does anyone know?

Marketing and PR can encompass a variety of subcategories or tactics. I've created this handy dandy image for you:

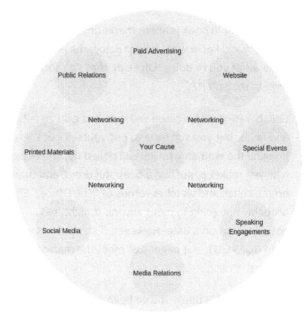

Paid Advertising

Public Relations

Website

Networking

Networking

Printed Materials

Your Cause

Special Events

Networking

Networking

Social Media

Speaking
Engagements

Media Relations

Let's dive in, shall we?

Networking

As a small business owner, possibly even a solopreneur,
the best marketing you will ever do is through
networking. In fact, one of my dreams is that the
networking conversation is forever changed by Cause
Marketing.

Think back to the last mixer you went to. You probably introduced yourself to a handful of people. And, I bet the conversation went like this:

"Hi, my name is (insert name here)."

"Hi, I'm Mark. What do you do?"

And then you told them. As you were talking, that person had a series of questions bouncing around in their head. "Can I sell my products or services to this person?," "Do I need what they are selling?" and "Do I like them enough to do business with them now or in the future?"

Sometimes, that conversation will progress and you'll move on to coffee to learn more about one another's businesses. Sometimes, you "suddenly" see someone you absolutely have to talk to and excuse yourself, tossing a business card over your shoulder as you walk away.

Now imagine this. You walk into a networking event and introduce yourself to someone.

"Hi, my name is (insert name here). What do you care about?"

Your conversation partner now spits out their watered-down gin and tonic. You've caught them off guard. They were all ready to tell you about their insurance business and find out about your network marketing company. Instead, they're wondering "What do I care about?"

117

You go on to explain to them how you were poor as a child and now everything you do in your business supports putting an end to childhood hunger. Or, you explain that you support animal rescue and already have pictures of your precious Fluffy McFluffernutter queued up on your phone, ready to show.

Now, the conversation has changed. The two of you are sharing stories about your beloved childhood pets. You are talking about that time you gave a homeless person your groceries or how your grandpappy earned a commendation for his service in the Army.

The conversation has changed. You'll get around to sharing what you do, but not until after you've built rapport and developed a relationship as human beings — not just potential customers or sources of referrals. Even cooler, your conversation partner is now wracking their brain thinking of all the people they know that love animals that they can connect you with.

The other tactics we're about to discuss will help get your name out there, but nothing is quite as powerful as a handshake and a story.

Public Relations

PR is an umbrella term that helps you develop a positive image with the community, the media, and your ideal customer. There are a number of ways to do this. We'll get into the largest way, Media Relations, in a moment. For now, think about the different organizations that you could speak to. Local clubs are always looking for speakers. You can provide free or low-cost trainings in your community, host events, sponsor a happy hour, etc.

Media Relations

Now it's time to dive into the media aspect of Public Relations. This includes print, radio, television, podcasts, YouTubers, etc. If you've never had any interaction with the press, don't be scared. They are more accessible than you think.

I sat down with Jess Todtfeld, one of the leading communication and media training authorities in the U.S. and the author of Media Secrets: A Media Training Crash Course. He shared the steps you'll need to take in order to court the media for your business, and a few strategies to stand out from the hundreds of requests they get every day.

1) Ask yourself why you want to get press. Is it for attention? Ego? Social Proof?

2) What do you want to make happen as a result of your press? Are you looking for the audience to make a buying decision that day? Do you want to gain favor with the public? Sometimes, the easiest thing you can do is offer them something free in exchange for their email address and an opt-in to your mailing list. You may not be selling anything at that moment, but you'll have the opportunity to build your tribe and market to them in the future.

3) Give. Give. Give. Offer something for free that is SO good, they can't even imagine how awesome your paid programs are.

4) Redefine the term "Plug." You've probably always seen "plugging" as telling the audience how amazing you are and how much they need your paid products. Instead, consider it this way:

P: Properly
L: Leverage
U: Ur (yes, he knows that's not how you spell "your")
G: Gift

When you are giving something away, be excited rather than nervous about making the pitch.

5) Ask for an Interview.

Yes, news desks, reporters, producers, and editors get A LOT of emails and phone calls requesting coverage. The good news is that they also NEED a lot of content to keep their shows or publications running. This means that if you have something newsworthy, and you present it properly, you've got a really good chance of getting attention.

Jess was a producer with NBC, ABC, and FOX for 13 years, so he knows what it's like on the other end of the phone or computer.

Press releases are no longer the best way to gain media favor. He suggests starting out with an email that has the following:

Start with a subject line that reads "Pitch:" or "Story:" and then provides an interesting hook about your situation.

Moving on to the body of the email, you'll need:
1) A big headline about your topic;
2) Who is available to talk on the topic;
3) Bullet points about what they would say;
4) Then you can add the traditional paragraphs from a press release (who is involved, what they do, where the event will be held, etc.).

The most important thing you can do is remember that these people are busy. Some of them are arranging new content every single day and they don't have time to dig through an email or press release to get to the good stuff.

Also, don't just *inform* the media. Jess laughed as he remembered a restaurant from New Mexico emailing him (in New York) to announce their grand opening. They weren't sending food and weren't prepared with a spokesperson to be interviewed. That's just a tease.

Ingredients + Tenacity = Media Success

If you'd like to learn more about Jess or buy his book, please visit https://www.successinmedia.com/

I've had my own experience with the media that you can use in your business, as well.

The first time I was on television, I had randomly reached out about a writing conference I was helping to organize. Imagine my surprise when a local television show invited me to be interviewed.

Imagine my fear.

Look, if you have a fear of public speaking or being on television or radio, you're not alone. It can be very scary. But it's also really cool. I was dating a guy with kids a few years ago. The kids saw me on television before they met me in real life. Needless to say, I was pretty much the coolest girlfriend their dad ever had.

Besides impressing potential step-kids, being on television can lend credibility to your business, your brand, and yourself. If you're afraid, join Toastmasters and overcome your fear.

If you're currently in the corner rocking and mumbling, "Oh heck no. Never gonna talk in public. Never gonna talk again," that's okay, too. Just make sure that someone in your organization is willing to speak on behalf of your company, your nonprofit, or your project.

I've probably been on television about 20 times now, and I won't say I've had *everything* happen, but there have certainly been some iffy situations. When you bring a live animal on TV, you are at their mercy. I had a Chihuahua lose her mind in the middle of a segment. Good times. I also went on television with a snake and lost my ability to speak for the entirety of the segment. Let's just say you shouldn't call me if you need a snake rescued.

Here's another tip: be nice.

Yup, I actually had to say that. For all the times that I've been on TV, there are many more times that I was supposed to be and it either got cut short or cancelled all together. Just in the last year, my segments were cut short because of a school shooting, the Mueller Report coming out, severe weather, and more.

When this happens to you, you'll have two choices. You can:

1) Say that you understand and accept an offer to come back on another day; or
2) Turn into a psycho and demand to talk to whoever is in charge while smashing camera equipment with your Hulk fists.

If you chose option # 2, please make your way to the nearest anger-management support group and get over yourself. When it comes to the media, things are always

123

happening. Breaking news is always going to trump your new smoothie flavor that's benefitting childhood cancer research. You know what else will take precedence? Paid advertisers.

As I mentioned before, "The Morning Blend" charges around $700 for a segment. Chances are that local shows in your community charge around the same. If you think that they are going to bump a paid segment in order to cover yours, you are sadly mistaken.

This is the world of media.

- Play by their rules
- Send them whatever they ask for
- Arrive early
- Be flexible and easy to work with
- Be nice when disappointments happen

So maybe you don't get to talk about your promotion or product *this time*. If you don't handle the disappointment well, you won't get to talk about your promotion or product *ever*.

Remember how I mentioned that networking is kind of important to business? It's important to media, as well. Develop relations. Foster those relationships. Treat those relationships like gold.

You'll want to create a media list to keep handy. Whenever you come into contact with someone who has the ability to book you, save their phone number and email address. If you are starting from scratch, contact the news desks, radio stations, and local publications. Ask them who you would pitch ideas to and what their preferred method of contact is.

Remember to be nice. Coworkers talk. If you flip your lid on the operator, don't expect the producer to embrace you with open arms.

Some outlets will still expect a full-blown press release, so it's helpful to have one written up. Then, you can just pull out the necessary info for your direct emails. (If you'd like an example, please visit www.dogoodtodobetter.com to download.)

Digital Marketing or Social Media

Social media is a bit like the Electoral College: some people claim to understand how it works, but most of us are navigating the landscape blindly.

So I decided to ask an expert. I spoke with Geoff Radcliffe, owner and strategist at Post Launch, a marketing agency in Las Vegas. He discussed what Cause Marketing looks like in his world.

"My job as a marketing strategist is to find my client's unique value in a very crowded world. The reality is that most people don't have much value to add."

That's what I've been saying! Remember how I mentioned that quickly responding to your clients, working hard and providing good customer service was just the bare minimum... see?!?

"When I work with clients," said Geoff, "I look for their '-est Factor.' Are they the fastest? The cheapest? The smartest at what they do? Cause Marketing allows you to be the most generous...est." (That's a new word and you can feel free to use it.)

In his experience, implementing a Cause-Marketing plan is more about putting in time than money. "People don't think they make enough of a margin or have the financial opportunity to engage in Cause Marketing. But, it's more important that they get involved."

Geoff likes to ask his clients what they're going to do when they get home after work. He usually gets a Cocker Spaniel-esque head tilt before he explains that they should head to a homeless shelter or an animal rescue to serve in some way. This is what will differentiate them from the next organization down the street.

"Businesses think that when you hire a marketing company, you write a check and things just magically get done. But we need something to work with. I provide the opportunity to get your message out... but you have to have a message to send. You can increase your Twitter followers, but if it doesn't lead to sales, who cares?"

Here are a few tips on how to fully embrace the power of Cause Marketing in your social media.

1) Take lots of pictures and videos. When you volunteer, get shots of the event, the space, your team, the fruits of your labor, and the population you are helping. Note: make sure it's okay for you to take pictures of people. If you are serving the homeless, they may not want to be photographed. If you are working with children, you'll need parental or guardian consent.

Your Smartphone will be sufficient for this. No need to spend money on expensive camera or video equipment.

2) Master the hashtag. Whenever you post to social media, use hashtags to insert yourself into an existing conversation. People that follow those hashtags will find you and (hopefully) be interested in what you have to say.

You'll want to utilize existing hashtags rather than making up your own (because no one is searching for that yet). You can find a hashtag generator on the web or as an app that will help you identify good ones to use. Example: https://www.all-hashtag.com/hashtag-generator.php (This is just one of many. We are not endorsing the use of this site or in any way connected to them).

If you are posting regularly (which you should be doing), you can use different hashtags each time.

3. Tag the organization you're volunteering with. This gives them more exposure and promotes awareness within your audience. You and your team should also tag them in your personal social media posts.

4. Ask your team and any adoring fans to comment on and share your posts.

Now that you are posting savvy, are you ready for a horrifying fact? Go ahead, sit down.

Facebook and Instagram only show you about 7% of what you follow. That means that if you have 100 friends (keeping math simple here, folks) you will only see posts from 7 of them. Yikes!

What the...? Why the...? Social media platforms want to make money, and they do this by selling advertising. If you're not buying ads, you need to find alternate ways to get noticed. Thankfully, the more engagement you have on a post, the more people will see it; so, Share baby, Share!

5. Use positive captions on your posts like, "It was so great getting the team together at (insert nonprofit here)." Then, give a line or two about what the organization does and how your followers can help.

6. Distribution throughout the platforms has become fairly similar, however, here's a guide for how to word your posts:

Twitter - Great for breaking news. "Come see the team on Saturday!"

Facebook - Recap what you've done. "We were here, we did cool things, join us next time."

Instagram - Good for brand recognition and improving employee morale.

LinkedIn - This is actually the lowest platform for content consumption. Unless someone spends the bulk of their day in an office, they are likely to check LinkedIn first thing in the morning and last thing at night. However, you should still share your activities on this platform, as people use it to research a company before they interview with it. If you are looking to woo better employees with your community involvement, this is the perfect place.

(Sidenote: if you serve on the board of a nonprofit or volunteer regularly, add it to your LinkedIn profile under experience.)

"Basically," Geoff said, "you have to create a regular schedule of volunteering to fully benefit from Cause Marketing. It needs to become a habit or it will become a burden."

If you'd like more information, please visit www.postlaunch.co or call (702)800-2131.

In order to give you more of a framework for your social media posts, I jumped on an Instagram Live with Erin Gargan King. She is the author of <u>Digital Persuasion</u> and teaches people how to "stop the scroll" in their social media.

She suggests that after a volunteer event with your team, you empower each employee to speak as an ambassador on behalf of your business rather than taking responsibility for the entire story.

Why?

Because every person has their own experience. Each participant sees the event through their own eyes and can communicate differently to your audience. (And if they share it on their personal pages, it will reach an even wider audience.) For example, King worked with one business who put on a clothing drive for a local organization. It was a huge undertaking with 50 people volunteering their time.

Whether they were packing up the boxes, handling registration, recruiting donors, or helping with marketing, each person was able to offer a different perspective on what the campaign meant to them.

Take the woman who had grown up with hoarders for parents. She'd spent her life pairing down her belongings and trying to "Marie Kondo her life." After the event, she was faced with the realization that while she was constantly purging her belongings, there were some people who had nothing of their own. She was able to provide the basics to help them feel like living, breathing human beings.

Another woman had spent her life battling body issues. She'd spend hours shopping trying to find an outfit that would make her feel confident as she stood in front of students or coworkers. She realized that not everyone was so fortunate to have options and felt good about helping others feel good about themselves.

As these unique experiences began to roll in, Erin was able to create a kaleidoscope narrative considerably more emotionally captivating than one that had been filtered through one person's eyes. The audience was now able to see themselves in the shoes of each of the volunteers.

Erin's got way more brilliance to share. Check her out at www.eringarganking.com.

Special Events

Hosting an event is a great way to not only get the community involved in your cause, but also get the media interested in it. You can start out by sending the press email we discussed earlier, just make sure that the event information is front and center and you make it very clear that you'd love to have someone attend the event. You'll also want to send a Media Advisory the day before (if you'd like an example, please visit www.dogoodtodobetter.com to download) and then follow up with a phone call to the news desk the morning of to see if they are available. Remember, there are a lot of things going on every day, and while they may agree to attend and cover your event, that might change at the last minute. Hope for the best, but be prepared for potential disappointment.

Printed Materials

Yes, we live in a digital world. However, there is still value to having marketing materials that you can hand someone when you're speaking with them. This can include a quick postcard or a tri-fold brochure that talks about your business, the cause you support, and how working with you will help out your chosen nonprofit.

The biggest key here is to talk about the cause. If your marketing materials don't mention the connection, they won't do you any good.

Website

Never forget that your website is often the first thing people read about you. If they were referred to you, found you through a Google search, or even if they saw you on television or at a speaking engagement, at some point, they are going to head over to your website to learn more about your services. At the very least, you need to have a page and a tab labeled Philanthropy or

Cause or Community Involvement. This page should explain what cause and nonprofit you've chosen, why, and how you are supporting them. There should be a brief explanation of what the nonprofit does and a link to their website.

If you'd like to bring the information front and center, add it to your homepage. Let visitors know at first glance that, not only are they solving their own problems by hiring you, they're also helping to fix a community problem.

Paid Advertising

If you have a budget for paid advertising, that's fantastic! This will give you the ability to carefully craft your message and then deliver it to whoever you want, whenever you want. Do your homework and see where your ideal customer hangs out. Make your decision based off of the audience, not the price. Reaching five good potential customers is much better than reaching 1,000 people who don't need or want what you've got to offer.

This can includes magazines, television, radio, billboards, placement on taxis or maybe even a sign twirler.

Guerilla Marketing

If you've never heard of this tactic before, you might be picturing those sign twirlers wearing furry costumes and taking banana breaks. Despite the name, guerilla marketing has nothing to do with apes. It's a term coined by Jay Conrad Levinson in his 1984 book <u>Guerilla Advertising</u> and it describes a style of marketing that is extremely unconventional, relatively inexpensive, and highly creative.

In <u>Win Win for the Greater Good</u>, Bruce W. Burtch talks about a "Super Crack" they created in the middle of Union Square in the San Francisco Bay area. This 60' by 10' photorealistic decal made it look as if Union Square had been cracked in an earthquake. This marketing tactic was part of a collaboration between the Red Cross and Pacific Gas & Electric, aimed at preparing San Franciscans for the eventual "Big One" predicted by scientists.

In 2005, Medecins du Monde utilized guerilla tactics to bring attention to the homeless in Paris. "Christened the 'tent city' initiative, the group distributed some 300 'two-second tents' to destitute Parisians sleeping outdoors. Equipped with the rapid-deploying tents (which didn't require poles or pins), the homeless gathered in small groups of eight to 10 along the Quai d'Austerlitz and the Canal Saint-Martin. The prefab shelter, which bore the Médecins du Monde logo, drew immediate attention to the number of homeless people in the area and provoked such incredible public outrage that the city was forced to act. A rare off-season government session was convened, and officials admitted that Paris' homeless shelters were vastly overcrowded. They immediately announced the allocation of nearly $10 million for emergency housing."[15]

I can't *not* share this...

Apparently, when GoldToe wanted to market their new clothing, they threw certain items on statues around New York — including a pair of undies on the famous bull statue.

https://blog.hubspot.com/marketing/guerilla-marketing-examples

Take advantage of any opportunity you have to encourage people to interact with your product or your campaign. I suppose you could also say "Grab a bull by the briefs"... I had to. Sorry.

Networking

Did I mention the importance of networking?

I know I did, but I really can't impress this upon you enough. No matter what avenues of marketing and PR you pursue, networking will help. Make it one of your life goals to always be able to say, "I know a guy!"

Chapter Twelve: Evaluating Your Campaign

Break out the party hats and hand out the kazoos. It's time to celebrate! I'm a fan of the Snoopy dance, but if you've got another way to get your celebration on, I respect and honor that.

Once you run out of champagne or sparkling apple cider it's time to ask an all-important question.

How did you do?

Selecting your nonprofit, carrying out your campaign, and sharing it with the world is all fine and good... but was it successful?

This is a tricky area because when you work with a nonprofit, success is not measured purely in profit or extra social media followers. In fact, the benefits of a Cause-Marketing campaign, or any type of community involvement, may not come immediately.

Think about the furniture store we discussed in Chapter Five. They actually *closed* their stores in order to help hurricane victims. They certainly didn't make any money during this time and probably lost quite a bit.

However, just put yourself in that situation for a moment. Hopefully, your consumer hat is nearby. You've just been through the most harrowing experience of your life. You may have been temporarily separated from your loved ones, you've likely lost your home and every single earthly possession you own except for the clothes on your back. You've probably spent at least a few nights at an emergency shelter sleeping on the floor or on a cot. You are scared, tired, hungry, and have no idea what the future will bring.

Then the employees of a local furniture store show up in a truck. They gather your family, including your fur kids, into the vehicle and usher you off to a safe, DRY, warm location, with actual furniture you can sleep on, and food.

Six months later, you are back in a home. Hopefully, your homeowners insurance has reimbursed you for the damage done to your property and possessions. It's time to buy furniture.

Where are you going to go?

If you answered anything other than, "That store that helped me when I was at my lowest point," you need to reevaluate your life.

You may not see the benefits of your good works for weeks, months, or even years to come. But they will come. I know I've got some analytical people reading this, and if I forgo the numbers, I may be hunted down.

So, here we go:

In Evolved Enterprise, the author talks about Elvis & Kresse, a company that turns reclaimed materials into bags, wallets, belts, and more, and then donates 50% of their profits to charities. Their site touts the following:

> Why do we make these donations? At Elvis & Kresse, we believe in the notion of good business: our business was established to solve environmental problems, waste problems in particular. We started with fire hoses and now reclaim more than 10 different materials. Beyond this, we also wanted to engage our material partners, our key stakeholders. Why not share, and why not see if more good could be done with the surplus of an already good business? Why not?
>
> In this sense, we are lucky. Most traditional businesses are only able to measure their success in one way - the bottom line. At Elvis & Kresse, we have two additional measure of success: how much waste we are able to divert from landfills and how much money we are able to give back to our charities, of which all three have equal importance to us.

This is why it's so incredibly important that your plan begins with what you are hoping to accomplish. If you don't know what you want to achieve, how will you know when you've gotten there?

Assuming you did your work in the beginning, you know the exact outcomes you were looking for and can judge based on those. If your goal was improved awareness of your brand, this could be measured by:

- How many website hits you received
- Media Impressions
- How much PR you received
- Social media follows and engagement

If you were looking to improve your sales, look for:

- Number and amount of sales during the promotion period vs. other time periods
- How much you invested in the project (advertising, man hours, product, etc.) vs. how much you made.

If you wanted to engage your employees and your customers:

- Number of volunteer hours completed
- Number of customers who purchased during the promotion and shared on social media

If your focus was on bringing awareness or funds to your cause:

- The amount you were able to donate.

- The number of volunteers the organization accrued during this time period.
- The media attention the charity received.
- The number of people or animals helped because of your collaboration. (Or the environmental effects if applicable).
- Concern and attention brought to the issue and the nonprofit.

Once you've taken a look at the different measures of success, ask yourself and your team if this collaboration was everything you hoped for and more. Ultimately, you (along with the nonprofit) are the only ones who can decide if this project was a success.

If you "succeeded," make sure to document what you did so that you can repeat it in the future.

If you missed the mark, don't beat yourself up too badly. You surely learned something in the process and can go into future collaborations (whether it's with the same group or another) armed with that knowledge to make the next one a bigger success.

Whether you reached your target goals or not, you probably created quite a bit of good for your business, the nonprofit, and the cause in general.

This is not a one-and-done type of program. If you want to make real impact in the community with your business, you'll constantly be testing the waters, adapting what has worked in the past to new situations, tweaking, improving, and learning. Focus on the good and you'll achieve your goals.

Chapter Thirteen: For the Nonprofit

Hey there, fellow nonprofit folks! I did promise that I'd get to you. Hopefully, you've actually been reading this whole book and haven't just flipped to this section.

For the past five years, I've been networking and asking for donations (both cash and in-kind) for the animal rescue. There are pros and cons to this method. Let's start out with the negatives so we can end on a positive note.

Cons

- You constantly feel like you're "begging"
- Your Facebook page too closely resembles the actual organization's
- For your birthday, people just assume that you want money donated to the nonprofit on your behalf, so you haven't seen a birthday present in years
- You constantly feel like you're "begging"
- Whenever people see you, they have some sort of supply for (insert the population you help). I once left a date with three boxes filled with Furminators. My rescue friends don't even ask questions anymore.
- If you run your own business, no one actually knows

- You've been hung up on, laughed at, and straight-up ignored (didn't realize an invisibility cape comes with the gig, did you?)
- Did I mention that you constantly feel like you're "begging"?

I remember a few years ago, I was walking around Superzoo, the pet industry event. For most vendors, it's cheaper to donate their products when the event is over, than to ship them to their next destination. So, I very nicely and respectfully stopped at each booth (there's only about a thousand of those bad boys) and asked:

1) Do you offer any discounts for nonprofits? We have a store that sells pet supplies to support our rescue efforts.

and

2) Did you intend to donate any of your product at the end of the event and, if so, do you already have an organization you are working with?

I'm going to make up some numbers to illustrate this. Let's say there are 1k vendors. I probably made it to about 300. About 275 of them were either taking their products with them or had already spoken to an organization. They were generally pretty nice and just told me they can't donate for one reason or another. Then there were 24 vendors that I actually got product from. That product was then used for the animals in our care, the community animals that we support, and one bag of treats was given to my dog... because if I didn't, she would disown me.

If you're keeping a tally, you'll recognize that there's one vendor left. I'm not giving you their name. Not because I'm afraid to get sued, but because I've blocked it from my memory. Here's how this went down:

"Hi sir, I'm with Hearts Alive Village, a 501(c)3 animal rescue here in Las Vegas. We have a pet supply store in town and I was wondering if you offer any discounts for nonprofits or will be donating any of your product from the show."

Here's when the man started laughing...

"No, sweetheart. We're capitalists."

So as not to get thrown out of the event, I bit my tongue until I was out of earshot and then called him many names. None of which were "capitalist."

Like everything else in life, there are positives as well.

Pros

- I've gone from an introvert to an extrovert
- I can talk to absolutely anyone
- I have no shame when it comes to asking for something for the animals (like seriously, no shame)

- I can hear "no" 275 times and still keep a smile on my face (please excuse me, I've just had an epiphany about sales and life in general...)
- I've learned the importance of storytelling and evoking an emotional connection with an "audience"
- I've gotten better at networking and building rapport and relationships
- I've had to find other ways to get what the rescue needs. Welcome to Cause Marketing.

If you've been doing fundraising for any period of time, you can probably relate.

The reason that I've written a special section just for you (though I've encouraged businesses to read this, as well), is because working for (or volunteering with) a nonprofit is hard. It's exhausting, energy sucking, not very lucrative, and amazing.

Congratulations. Your passion is so strong, that you toil day in and day out for little to no money, just so you can see the smile on kid's faces, the appreciation from the homeless, a tail wag from an animal saved, or whatever sign of success you see from your population.

There's one thing that you need to remember as you go about your fundraising... not everyone shares your passion.

You may be willing to forgo family vacations and dye your hair at home instead of at the salon. You may be okay with driving an old, beat-up car instead of trading it in every three years for the latest and greatest. However, not everyone is.

I know it's hard to hear. I can't possibly comprehend that anyone doesn't care about animals. Yet, I'm constantly presented with the evidence. You approach an individual or a business with all the excitement of someone who knows the joy of saving a life, and you are met with all the excitement of someone who has just answered their 459th telemarketing call in one hour.

Businesses have to make money. If they don't, they can't pay their people, they can't order supplies, they can't pay the rent for their offices, and their employees won't be able to keep a roof over their heads and food on their families' plates.

You may wander across a few businesses that are rolling in the moolah and can "make it rain" for every charity that approaches them. (And if you do, can you call me?) But, in order to get help from the rest of the businesses, you'll need to constantly consider the WIIFM concept. If you've never been in sales, this stands for "What's In It For Me?"

When you are asking an individual for a donation, you're appealing to their desire to feel good (and maybe get a tax exemption); but when you talk to a business, you need to show them how helping you is actually going to help them.

How do you do that?

Make yourself attractive to businesses by:

Having a strong social media footprint

Whatever social media avenues you choose to use, put some effort in to it. While you may not be a national brand with millions of followers, having 10k is better than having ten.

Maintaining a good reputation

Just like a business has to focus on their brand and reputation, you do as well. The best advice I can give here?

- Keep your nose clean
- Be transparent about your dealings
- Stay positive
- Avoid bashing anyone in the community... even if they are part of the problem, yet claim to be part of the solution
- Think twice, post once on social media or anywhere else you have a footprint

Being clear about what you do and how you help the community

If you don't know what you do, how do you expect anyone else to understand and get excited? Craft a great origin story (why you do what you do) and plenty of success stories (who you've helped and how) and be prepared to tell them to anyone who will listen.

In Good Works, the authors said,

> Causes most often supported through these (marketing and corporate social) initiatives are those that contribute to *community health* (i.e., AIDS prevention, early detection for breast cancer, timely immunizations); *safety* (i.e., designated drive programs, crime prevention, use of car safety restraints); *education* (i.e., literacy, computers for schools, special needs education); *employment* (i.e., job training, hiring practices, plant locations); the *environment* (i.e., recycling, elimination of the use of harmful chemicals, reduced packaging); *community and economic development* (i.e., low-interest housing loans, mentoring entrepreneurs); and *other basic human needs and desires* (i.e., hunger, homelessness, protecting animal rights, exercising voting privileges, anti-discrimination).

Where does your organization fit in? Know exactly what you do so you can sell it when given the opportunity.

In addition, everyone that "represents" your organization should be able to communicate your mission, your programs, your vision, and your successes. I put represents in quotation marks because if you have a volunteer working an event for you, they should be able to handle questions. They should also know when to **not** handle them. Make sure everyone knows who handles media inquiries, and any other "official" conversations, and can direct interested parties to them.

Being proud of who you are and know that you bring value to the table

I know it feels like you've been begging, but stand up straight and smile. You are changing the world. You have value (and, gosh darn it, people like you). Just like I advised businesses to do an inventory, your organization should do one, as well. Some of the "assets" you might not even realize you have:

- Real estate - Not just physical space, you've also got a website, marketing materials, etc.
- Events- You can get butts in seats.
- Social Media - You have reach!
- Database/Mailing List - If you're not keeping one now (and sending out newsletters), it's never too late to start.
- Email Signature - sound silly? Here's why it's not. A few years ago, my email signature included my title for Hearts Alive Village with a link to the website and my Area Director title for Toastmasters along with a link to our site. I contacted someone at United Way with questions about the Federal Campaign. He saw

the Toastmaster's connection and asked around in the animal community about the rescue (remember how important reputation is???). He then called me to walk me through the application. We're now friends and have worked together on numerous projects. Email signatures are important!

Being appreciative

Did your mom make you write "Thank you" notes when you got a gift from someone? Your mom was a genius. Continue the tradition by saying thank you in person, creating a plaque, announcing someone's support on social media, creating a banner with their logo for your events, baking brownies. Whatever it is, be grateful. They didn't *have* to help you. And if you're not appreciative, you can be sure they won't do it again.

Providing a tour and presentation to educate the business and get them excited to help

If you have a facility, offices, events, etc., invite potential collaborators to come visit. Show them what you do. If you're working with a store, go to them. Prepare a presentation that will educate them on what your organization does, get them excited about all the good that's been done, and make them feel like a part of the team.

Being easy to work with

I know this last one seems pretty obvious, but I'm constantly amazed by how much the obvious gets overlooked. I'll give you an example.

Last summer, an e-cig company, E-Cig Distributors, approached our rescue with their Dog Days of Summer campaign. For one day, a percentage of all purchases would be donated to our rescue. I asked them what they needed to proceed and they said, "your logo, 501(c)3 paperwork, and someone to take pictures when we deliver the check."

Done!

Three months later, the company came in to our adoption center, with a comically large $3k+ check in hand. I shook the marketing woman's hand and then gave her a huge hug.

"Thank you so much for doing this! We can save so many more lives now," I said while handing her a puppy to cuddle.

"Thank you for being so easy to work with," she said. "You'd be amazed how hard it is to work with nonprofits sometimes. Some are even nasty."

Umm what? She asked for three things and gave us $3k. It really begs the question... HOW ARE NONPROFITS MAKING IT DIFFICULT TO WORK WITH THEMSELVES?!?

I'm sorry to yell there; I just seriously don't understand. I get it, you're strapped for time. I know you've got nine million things to do and no one else to do it. However, when someone wants to give you money... please make it easy for them to do so.

All right, I'm calm again now. And this is a perfect segue into what you can and can't do.

Remember I mentioned Ed Chansky, that attorney that I sat down with when I was researching for this book? He taught me A LOT about the nonprofit's role in Cause Marketing.

I was under the impression that Cause Marketing was a partnership between a business and a nonprofit - like prancing through a field of daisies with their arms linked while butterflies flitted around their heads.

Yeah. No.

First, never say the word "partnership" in front of an attorney. They breathe fire. (Just kidding, he was wonderful!). A legal partnership is a business entity with a sharing of profit and loss. If you've noticed, I've been very careful to only use the word "collaboration" throughout this book... that's why.

Second, as a nonprofit, your job is basically to sit back and look pretty. Okay, it's a little more involved than that. Note: Please be advised that this should not be taken as legal or tax advice. I am neither a lawyer, nor an accountant... nor did I sleep at a Holiday Inn Express last night. Please consult a professional. Here goes:

You can be an active *collaborator* or a passive *collaborator*. Active means that you are actively promoting their product or service through your channels. If you do this, you must be careful not to muddy the waters between Acknowledgment and Advertising.

If you'd like to make your ears bleed, here's the IRS regulation governing it: https://www.govinfo.gov/content/pkg/CFR-2009-title26-vol7/pdf/CFR-2009-title26-vol7-sec1-513-4.pdf

If you'd rather not require smelling salts, here's a synopsis:

Acknowledgement is "Thank you to _____ for their support. Please visit their website to learn how they help."

Advertising is making qualitative statements endorsing the company, making value statements about their products, and/or inducing your audience to buy from them. "Please purchase widgets from _____. They have the best widgets in town and they'll donate a percentage of each purchase to our organization."

Now, it's okay to advertise for them (although if more than 25% of your income comes from these situations, it could threaten your charitable status). However, there's this ugly little creature out there called a UBIT. It's not a gremlin, zombie, or cousin of the hobbit. The UBIT is an Unrelated Business Income Tax. It's what happens when you start making claims about your *collaborators* and end up becoming a marketing or ad agency for them. If you do, you pay tax on the service you provided. In case you missed it up above, please note that I am not an attorney or an accountant. All questions should be directed to a professional.

This UBIT isn't necessarily a bad thing. If you bring in hundreds of thousands of dollars on a promotion, you probably wouldn't mind paying a bit of tax. It's just something I want you to be aware of so you can enter into all *collaborations* with your eyes open. Talk to an attorney, talk to a tax advisor, talk to your mom. Just make sure you know what you're doing.

Approach Them

This isn't a 1950's dance. You don't have to stand in the corner hoping and praying that one of the "cool kids" will ask you to dance. Create a "wishlist" of businesses that you'd like to collaborate with and then approach them. Your cause and your organization may be just what they were looking for.

Most importantly...

Protect Yourself

Hopefully, all of the people you come into contact with during your lifetime will be upstanding, honest, good people. However, you're likely to encounter a dud here and there. Your organization has a mission and if you let a company put you in an uncomfortable position, you'll jeopardize that mission.

Even if you do not engage in any "active marketing" for the business, you may think that you are the only one on the receiving end of the benefits. While you will gain money and exposure from this collaboration, the business to whom you lend your name and logo will get something known as the "halo effect." Basically, they will be seen in a positive light by their potential customers.

Please don't underestimate the value that you bring to this situation. And, please, be careful who you get into bed with. If they have been known for "shifty" business, represent an industry that you'd rather not be associated with, or make your skin crawl when you meet them... steer clear. I don't mean to harp, but reputation is everything. Don't allow any business to cheapen your reputation just to get a few dollars donated. In the end, it's not worth the repercussions.

When done properly, Cause Marketing and working with businesses can be an excellent addition to your fundraising plan. On the next page, you'll see an Action Plan that you can use to get started.

9 Step Action Plan

- ☐ Understand Your Why
- ☐ Inventory Your Business
- ☐ Select Your Cause and Find a Nonprofit
- ☐ Choose Your Strategy
- ☐ Outline Your Campaign
- ☐ Craft Your Story
- ☐ Create Your Marketing Plan
- ☐ Put Your Plan in Motion
- ☐ Evaluate Your Campaign

Download a checklist at:
www.dogoodtodobetter.com

Section Three:

Next Steps

Chapter 14: Certification

In Chapter Four we discussed how some people are hesitant to give or purchase during a Cause-Marketing campaign because they don't believe that the charity actually sees the money.

I get it. One of the biggest challenges regarding Cause Marketing, or any type of promotion that incorporates a nonprofit, is that there's no governing body. There's no organization that will oversee the collaboration and confirm that, indeed, the business did raise funds on behalf of the nonprofit AND the charity actually received the funds.

Until now.

I'm currently working on a certification program.

If you've ever picked up a product and looked for the leaping bunny symbol that ensures no animals were harmed during its manufacturing or testing, or checked to make sure that your purchase was part of the Sustainable Forestry Initiative, you understand the value of third-party oversight.

Our goal is to create a symbol that will be synonymous with businesses that are doing good in our communities. Businesses can display this symbol proudly on their doors, websites, marketing materials, and business cards, and consumers can rest easy knowing that their charitable contributions and purchases are actually making it to their intended destinations.

For more information about certification, please visit https://www.sherylgreenspeaks.com/certification-program/

Chapter 15: Consulting

If you've read this book and really absorbed the information, you should have a good handle on how to incorporate Cause Marketing, or giving forward, into your business.

Sometimes though, it's nice to have someone personally guiding you along the way. If you'd like more assistance in selecting a charity and implementing a program in your business, I'd love to help.

I've got a consulting/video course combination if you're more comfortable working through the program more independently and consulting packages for one-on-one guidance.

Still not sure that Cause Marketing is right for you? If you're willing to answer a quick survey about your business, I'll give you a free 30-minute phone call where you can ask me anything (about Cause Marketing... or my dog).

Please contact me at sheryl@sherylgreenspeaks.com for more information.

Conclusion

There's something different in the air these days. I feel it when I talk to business leaders, give speeches at High School and college campuses, and engage in conversations with fellow patrons at coffee shops. People are hungry for success. That's nothing new. What's changed is the definition of that success. Increasingly, the quest for success is not the same as the quest for status and money. The definition has broadened to include contributing something to the world and living and working on one's own terms.
- Blake Mycoskie

The more and more I researched for this book, the more I realized that there are wonderful things happening in the world. Businesses and individuals are waking up to the challenges that we face as a society, and for the most part, they are banding together to affect real change.

I hope that this book has been helpful for you. I hope that you have been able to identify a cause and a charity that are close to your heart, and learned how you can leverage your support to improve your business.

As I mentioned before, I grew up in a Jewish household where I basically had to learn some Yiddish just to survive. Every so often, a Yiddish word will pop into my head instead of the English version.

As I sit here writing, the word "mensch" is bouncing around in my brain. A mensch is a person of integrity and honor. This is the sentiment I'd like to leave you with today.

Whether you are a business owner, a sales person, a nonprofit employee, or someone who picked this book up in a coffee shop and had nothing better to read, be a good person. Serve your community, speak for those who have no voice, and strive to leave this planet a little bit better than how you found it.

"Service is the rent we pay for the privilege of living on this earth." - Shirley Chisholm

Thank you,

Sheryl Green

About the Author

Sheryl Green is a New York native living and thawing in Las Vegas since 2008. After spending several years fundraising for non-profits, Sheryl Green got tired of begging for money. Knowing that there must be a better way to raise the funds the organizations needed, she discovered Cause Marketing. She now teaches businesses how to leverage the power of doing good to improve their visibility, favorability, and profitability.

Sheryl holds a Master's Degree in Psychology and has worked in Customer Service, Public Relations, Education, and the Non-Profit world. A passionate animal advocate, she serves as the Director of Communications and Cuddling for Hearts Alive Village and is the co-founder of the Cause Marketing Chamber of Commerce.

She is the author of <u>Surviving to Thriving: How to Overcome Setbacks and Rock Your Life</u>, <u>Once Upon a Bottom Line: Harnessing the Power of Storytelling in Sales</u>, <u>Book Writing for Busy People</u>, and <u>Do Good to Do Better: The Small Business Guide to Growing your Business by Helping Nonprofits</u>.

In her spare time, she likes to read, travel, hike with her Beagle/Lab mix Akasha, and do yoga (also sometimes involving Akasha).

To book Sheryl, visit: www.sherylgreenspeaks.com.

Notes

1. http://www.psaresearch.com/bib9827.html (18)

2. https://www.edelman.com/news-awards/two-thirds-consumers-worldwide-now-buy-beliefs (26)

3. https://news.gallup.com/poll/180404/gallup-daily-employee-engagement.aspx (39)

4. https://blog.octanner.com/engagement/want-happier- more-engaged-employees-give-back-this-season (40)

5. http://www.conecomm.com/research-blog/2016-millennial-employee-engagement-study (41)

6. https://thehustle.co/Farming-hazelnuts-Nutella-working-conditions/ (54)

7. https://www.washingtonpost.com/news/on-leadership/wp/2018/03/06/dicks-sporting-goods-took-a-stand-on-gun-sales-and-made-a-big-statement/?noredirect=on&utm_term=.93971edd3dbb (54)

8. https://www.usatoday.com/story/money/retail/2018/0 5/17/dicks-sporting-goods-hurt-by-gun-owners-boycott/34999931/ (5)

9. https://www.npr.org/2019/02/12/691999347/soul-searching-after-parkland-dicks-ceo-embraces- tougher-stance-on-guns (55)

10. https://www.cbsnews.com/news/houston-businessman-jim-mcingvale-opens-furniture-stores- to-evacuees/ (64)

11. https://contentmarketinginstitute.com/2019/06/ca use-marketing-wrong/#.XRYlQKOlBG0.twitter (74)

12. https://www.shrm.org/hr-today/trends-and-forecasting/research-and-surveys/Documents/2018%20Employee%20Benefits%20Report.pdf (107)

13. https://www.apple.com/newsroom/2019/01/out- of-a-culture-of-giving-a-world-of-difference/ (97)

14. https://www.insidephilanthropy.com/home/2019/ 2/4/titos-employees-spread-the-love-to-choice- charities (98)

15.http://www.creativeguerrillamarketing.com/guerrilla -marketing/6-great-guerrilla-marketing-campaigns/(134)

16. https://cfda.com/resources/sustainability-resources/detail/the-consumer-study-from-marketing-to-mattering-2014-by-the-un-glbal-compact-accenture-ceoin-collaboration-with-havas-media-repurpose (31)

References

Austin, James E. *The Collaboration Challenge*. San Francisco: Jossey-Bass Publishers, 2000.

Butler-Madden, Carolyn. *Path to Purpose*. Australia: Major Street Publishing, 2017.

Burtch, Bruce. *Win Win for the Greater Good*. 2013.

Hirsch, Peter L. and Robert B. Gordon. *Global Cause Marketing*. 2013.

Kotler, Philip, David Hessekiel, and Nancy R. Lee. *Good Works!*. Hoboken: John Wiley & Sons, Inc. 2012.

Linial, Peggy. *Marketing From the Heart*. Scottsdale: Morpheus Publications. 2003.

Mycoskie, Blake. *Start Something That Matters*. Random House Audio. 2011.

Silver, Yanik. *Evolved Enterprise*. Ideapress Publishing. 2015.

Waters, Joe and Joanna MacDonald. *Cause Marketing for Dummies*. Hoboken: Wiley Publishing, Inc. 2011.